KT-488-517

KT-488-517

THE MARSHALL GUIDE TO
ANTIQUE
CHINA & SILVER

THE MARSHALL GUIDE TO
ANTIQUE
CHINA & SILVER

AN ILLUSTRATED GUIDE TO TABLEWARE, IDENTIFYING PERIOD, DETAIL AND DESIGN

TIM FORREST
CONSULTING EDITOR PAUL ATTERBURY

MARSHALL PUBLISHING • LONDON

A Marshall Edition
Conceived, edited and designed by
Marshall Editions Ltd
170 Piccadilly
London W1V 9DD

First published in the UK in 1998 by
Marshall Publishing Ltd

Copyright © 1998 Marshall Editions
Developments Limited

All rights reserved including the right of
reproduction in whole or in part in any form.

ISBN 1-84028-064-6

PROJECT EDITOR Theresa Lane
DESIGN Poppy Jenkins
PICTURE EDITOR Elizabeth Loving
PICTURE MANAGER Zilda Tandy
RESEARCH James Rankin
DTP EDITORS Mary Pickles, Lesley Gilbert
MANAGING EDITOR Lindsay McTeague
EDITORIAL COORDINATOR Rebecca Clunes
ART DIRECTOR Sean Keogh
EDITORIAL DIRECTOR Sophie Collins
PRODUCTION Nikki Ingram
Origination in Singapore by HBM Print
Printed and bound in Italy
by New Interlitho Spa, Milan

*The splendid dining table in the Banqueting Room
in the Brighton Pavilion is set with a dessert
service, together with elaborate candelabras and
centrepieces. It was common for the Prince Regent
to dine with 30 or more guests at a time, and the
menu sometimes had as many as 60 dishes.*

CONTENTS

INTRODUCTION

Anyone who has visited or seen photographs of the dining room at the Hillwood Museum in Washington, D.C., the former home of Mrs Merriweather Post – an American heiress renowned for her hospitality – will know how spectacular a table laid with antique china and silver can look.

This book endeavours to introduce the silver and ceramic tablewares that have been used at the dining table since the 16th century and to show the features that help identify their style, date, manufacturer and country of origin. The chosen pieces range from the relatively common to the rare, but all have been selected to explain and illustrate how an item can be judged. The book also provides an introduction to how the tablewares were used by our ancestors during meals.

The wealth of silver and ceramic tablewares made in Europe, Great Britain and the United States from the 16th century onward is a substantial subject for any book. Although glass came to be used at the dining table from the 17th century onward, it is a subject worthy of a book of its own and has not been included here.

Collecting silver or ceramic tablewares is an exciting interest to pursue because there are still many examples to be found, either as individual pieces or as a set or part of a set, and you can buy them either to use at your table or for display. In fact, Mrs Post regularly used valuable French and Russian porcelain when entertaining her guests. If you decide to use a valuable piece instead of display it, you should take into consideration that you may risk damaging it.

Before buying a piece or set, make sure it is one that you like and want to see in your home. Look for damage or signs of repair, which will reduce the value of the piece. Items sold as a pair or set, and ones that are in their original cases, will be worth more than those sold alone.

The cutlery and ceramics you collect do not necessarily have to be old to be a good investment. Many items from the 1930s onward are now keenly sought after, especially if they were designed by a notable architect, artist or designer – and they may well prove to be the antiques of the future.

GEORGE II TEA CADDIES AND SUGAR BOWL
Because tea was expensive, tea caddies were locked in a case. The upside-down pear shape of the caddies is typically rococo, as is the ornate decoration of chased scrolls and scalework. The silverware was made in 1750, but the case was made at a later date.

NAPLES ICE PAIL, COVER AND LINER
The way in which history can inspire a revival of a style is apparent on this late 18th-century neoclassical ice pail, which was influenced by excavations at Pompeii and Herculaneum. The main body is decorated with classical figures, the handle is adorned with lion masks and the base has anthemion decoration.

HOW TO USE THIS BOOK

The information in this book is presented in three different ways. Each chapter begins with an annotated photograph of a table setting to demonstrate how the wares in the chapter would have been used at the table. Also within the book are special feature pages that provide a focus on specific items such as cutlery. This at-a-glance chronological reference illustrates how styles and the form of these items have changed throughout history.

The rest of the book is dedicated to two-page treatments of tableware. There is usually a main piece that is typical of the style or period under discussion, or of interest because of its aesthetic appeal or history, or because it is by a renowned designer. This piece is analysed in detail, and features of interest are pinpointed in words and secondary images. Alongside it are complementary pieces which demonstrate the development of a style or offer alternative interpretations of it.

Brief introduction to the period the chapter covers.

Useful terms appropriate to the chapter.

A full-colour photograph of a table setting representing how the wares were used during the period; captions provide explanations.

Charts offer myriad variations in design and stylistic details.

Labels identify when and where items were popular.

Variations show related wares.

Details pinpoint stylistic or constructional features.

Captions describe details of the piece and its manufacture.

Large full-colour photograph of a beautiful or important example of the subject under discussion.

Complementary images show national or regional variations, or works in a similar style by different makers.

Text offers an introduction to a type of tableware and its period.

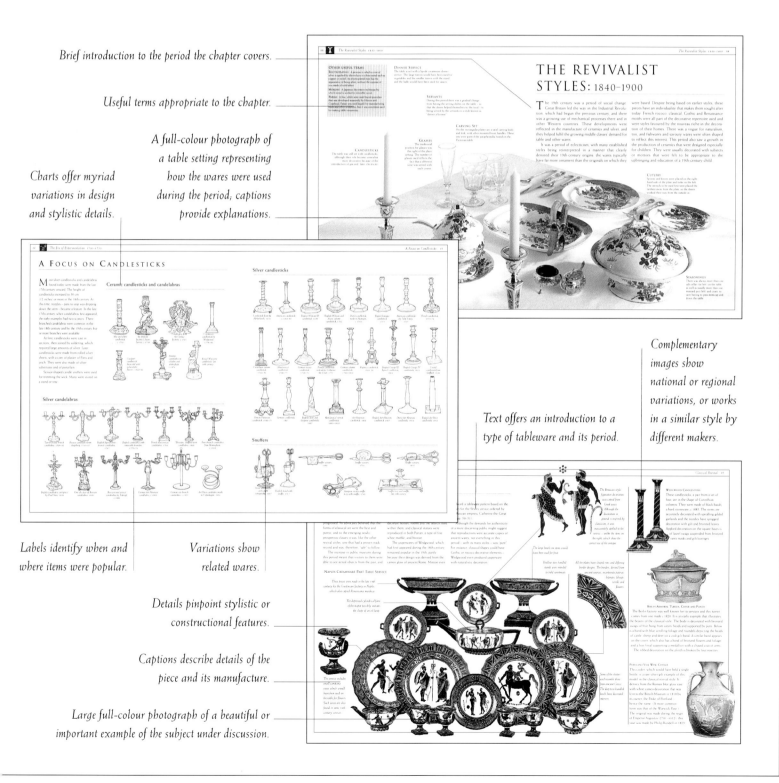

A BRIEF HISTORY OF EATING

The story of eating is as old as humankind, but since most of the ceramic and silver tablewares that have survived date from the 16th century onward, this is the point at which this history will begin. The idea of communal eating in the great hall of a house or castle, which prevailed earlier, continued into the 16th century, but the family preferred to eat in a smaller, more domestic setting on their own, only joining their household on special occasions in the hall. Most people had an early breakfast, between 6:00 am and 7:00 am, with an early dinner being served around 2:00 pm.

Until the end of the 18th century, cooks were dependent upon locally produced foodstuffs for their ingredients, and because meat could not be kept fresh for long it was usually salted to extend the length of time it could be stored. The voyages of exploration brought new foodstuffs to Great Britain and Europe and the increasing interrelations between continental countries saw the introduction of new food delicacies such as several varieties of beans – including the kidney bean, lima bean, scarlet runner and string bean – and potatoes and sweet potatoes.

FAMILY SAYING GRACE BEFORE A MEAL
This painting by Gortzuis Geldrop (1553–1618) shows a family praying at the table before eating their meal. The food is already on the table, which is set with pewter plates, spoons and knives, as well as napkins. There is also a stoneware jug and the standing salt. The handle on the serving fork is of a style popular in Flanders at this period.

THE OYSTER LUNCH

Painted by Jean François de Troy (1679–1752), the scene shows a party of men at lunch. The table is set with silver plates and dishes, trencher salt cellars and glass coolers. The tablecloth was also used as napkins in England at this time.

THE BREAKFAST

This 1842 engraving by J. Bouvier of a painting by William Tayler (1809–1892) was published as plate 3 in *Anglo-Indians*. A young British couple is taking breakfast, with their servants in attendance. The ex-colonials brought Indian recipes back with them, such as the one for kedgeree, a breakfast favourite.

Among the items on the table was the wooden trencher, on which food was served or cut, and it incorporated a smaller space for salt – hence the term "trencher" for "dished" salts. For the wealthy, silver was the norm, and their tables were set with silver vessels, including the large bell-shaped salts – or so-called great salts – that were popular in this period. Salt was then a highly valued substance, and only one great salt was placed on the table. In fact, the importance of salt can perhaps best be realized when it is considered that the word salary comes from the Latin word for salt, *sal*, because salt was part of the payment received by the soldiers of imperial Rome. As a preservative of meat, salt was regarded as an important trading commodity.

Tablewares made of pewter and silver were used for eating and drinking. Pottery was also used for drinking vessels and Venetian glass was introduced. Silver that was not being used was displayed on court cupboards as a symbol of wealth – a custom that has lasted through to the 20th century. Although the word banquet today means a sumptuous somewhat formal meal, to the Tudors it was used to describe an elaborate dessert course that was usually served in another room or even a banqueting pavilion, either on the roof, such as at Longleat House in Wiltshire, or in the garden or park. Sugar figures were featured among the often lavish display of symmetrically arranged dishes; indeed, the workshop of the great sculptor Giambologna is recorded as making sugar figures for weddings of members of the Medici family.

THE 17TH CENTURY

Pewter continued to be used for eating wares but because it is a softer material than silver, the surfaces of plates were easily scored by knives, so it needed constant care and attention. The ceramic industries were growing at the time and the increased use of slipwares and delft helped alleviate that problem. The use of great salts also declined in popularity, and they were replaced by individual salt cellars. The range of foodstuffs continued to expand with new discoveries brought back from the Far East and the American colonies. Perhaps the most important new feature was the significant role played by tea, chocolate and coffee in social life – this certainly spawned a whole new series of vessels for their preparation and consumption.

New continental eating habits were introduced to Great Britain by the royalists, who returned to the country from Europe with King Charles II in 1660. During the latter half of the century the fork became an established part of the cutlery. Prior to that the knife and spoon had been the only cutlery used, and the knife had a pointed blade to spear the food and bring it to the mouth. With the fork taking over the role of food carrier, the blade of the knife was now wider.

By the end of the 17th century, increased commerce with China saw a trade in which Chinese porcelain tablewares and teawares were imported in vast quantities to meet Western demand. The imported china was particularly popular as it was far more durable than homemade wares and better able to withstand the temperatures of hot beverages.

THE 18TH CENTURY

The Chinese export trade flourished well into the 18th century, despite the fact that Western factories were now producing wares in both hard- and soft-paste porcelain. Silver featured prominently among tablewares, and items ranging from plates to ornate tureens and centrepieces were produced. In the 18th century food was served in a way known as *table à la française*. The table was laid for each course with the relevant dishes and tureens set in the centre of the table so that diners could help themselves and their neighbours. This happened for each of the two main courses, which had numerous dishes, before the dessert course was introduced in all its lavish finery. The first course would include soup, fish and meat, while the second consisted of a mixture of savoury and sweet dishes, including fish and meat once more.

Kitchens were usually situated some distance away from the dining room, even in a separate wing, to prevent the smell of the food from permeating the main part of the house. Despite the use of dish warmers and other such items, the food cannot have been very hot by the time it reached the diner's plate. Dinner, by the end of the century, was served in the early evening, but it was still a lengthy meal, often lasting several hours, and there was also a "light" supper before retiring. Cookery books, which proliferated in the 18th century, not only included menus but also table plans showing how the tables should be set. Mrs Beeton, in her books toward the end of the 19th century, took up this idea. As well as the necessary dishes, it was usual for the table to be decorated down the centre with a host of figures, either made of sugar or, as became more common, porcelain. Vases, silver or porcelain baskets for sweetmeats and candelabras were also featured.

THE 19TH CENTURY

Although the 19th century saw the continuing use of the dining arrangement from the previous century, a new form of service was introduced in France – reputedly by a Russian ambassador – and it replaced the *table à la française* style of eating. Instead of the dishes being set on the table, they were now placed on the sideboard and side tables and the dishes were served by the servants, in a style known as *table à la russe*. During this century two new mealtimes, lunch and afternoon tea, assumed prominence in polite society and were used as a way of entertaining. They were necessary meals, for by now dinner was often not served until 8:30 pm or later.

Dinners were still substantial meals and, as in earlier periods, accompanied by large amounts of alcohol – a different wine was served with each course. The Victorian gentleman, however, did

DARBY AND JOAN

In this painting by Walter Dendy Sadler (1854–1923), an elderly couple toast each other – portraits of them in their younger days are on the wall behind them. The scene emphasizes the formality of dining in the 19th century, with the couple at opposite ends of the table and the large silver epergne at the centre filled with flowers.

DINNER TABLE FROM MRS BEETON

This table setting, from the 1907 edition of Mrs Beeton's famous cookery book, is somewhat old fashioned for the time as it depicts a *table à la française*. All the serving dishes are on the table for the first course but will only be used after the soup, seen at the end, has been served. The elaborate central floral display is typical of the period.

not drink to the same degree as his forebears. The idea of eating when travelling was not a new concept, but during the 19th century the habit of going out for a meal became more acceptable, especially in Europe, and the development of grand hotels had made it respectable by the early years of the 20th century.

THE 20TH CENTURY

The amount of differing dishes in a meal diminished to a more sensible level in the 20th century. The ever-increasing growth of technology and the development in the production of frozen and brand-name foods meant that a wider segment of the population had the possibility of eating better meals. The growth of mass production brought decorative tablewares to all levels of society. World War II in many ways swept away the old order and there was the concept of a New Age. Servants were now a thing of the past, whereas before the war even middle-class households would have had a maid or cook to help in the house. Life became more informal and labour-saving gadgets in the kitchen made life more tolerable for even those who had never previously had to cook.

The methods of preparing food expanded as different cultures mixed and cookery books on most of the world's cuisines became available, as well as the exotic ingredients for many of the recipes. Despite the new informality, there was a preoccupation with table settings for entertaining. Modern designs were popular, but traditional tablewares continued to find favour – even an 18th-century nobleman's table can be re-created. It seems there will always be room for traditional styles to coexist with the new, which may in time come to be regarded as enduring pieces themselves.

FIVE O'CLOCK

In this painting by George Dunlop Leslie (1835–1921), a lady is seated in the garden with a table from the drawing room beside her. On it is a tray with a coffee pot and cups and saucers. Tea or coffee was usually taken at around 5:00 in the afternoon because this was midway between lunch and dinner.

USEFUL TERMS

Decorative techniques and ornaments

Fluting

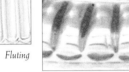
Gadrooning

Famille rose

Gilding

En grisaille

Finial

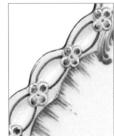
Feuille de choux

Putto

ACANTHUS *A leaf pattern widely used in classical antiquity and revived in the late 18th century as an ornamental motif.*

AESTHETIC MOVEMENT *A precursor to Art Nouveau, a decorative style in Great Britain and the United States that was influenced by decoration on Japanese objects. It flourished only briefly, c.1870–80.*

ALLOY *A metal created by melting together two or more elements, such as copper, tin and zinc, creating a stronger material. For example, sterling silver contains some copper or other base metal to help strengthen it. Bronze and pewter are two metals used in tablewares that are made in this way.*

ANTHEMION *Stylized flower motif based on honeysuckle and derived from classical Greek ornament. It is often found on 18th- and 19th-century silverware.*

ANTIMONY *Used in a variety of alloys, including pewter, a metallic element that has hardening properties.*

APPLIED DECORATION *Ornamentation that is first made, then attached to the body of the ware: on ceramics, often with a slip, or liquid clay; on metals, they are typically soldered in place.*

ARCADING *A decorative feature that takes the form of a series of rounded arches.*

ARMORIAL *A full coat of arms or designs incorporating heraldic symbols used to decorate a ware; they are often found on Chinese export and European porcelain and on silverware.*

ART DECO *A modernist style that affected the decorative arts from the 1920s to the 1930s. The name is an abbreviation for the French arts décoratifs.*

ART NOUVEAU *A style recognizable by its flowing lines, curves and asymmetry. Flower and leaf motifs were common in this style, which flourished from the 1880s to World War I.*

ARTS AND CRAFTS MOVEMENT *A period in the late 19th to early 20th centuries in which designers moved away from the ornate to simple decoration; wares were hand-made rather than machine made. It floundered in Great Britain after 1900 and in the United States and Europe after World War I.*

BALUSTER *A turned column with a curving shape used in furniture, for example, a table leg. The form was imitated in ceramics and silverware, as can be seen in some early coffee pots and candlesticks.*

BASE METAL *A non-precious metal, such as copper, iron, lead and tin, or one of their alloys, including pewter, bronze and German silver.*

BAT PRINTING *An 18th-century process in which a delicate pattern was applied on top of a ceramic glaze. A design was printed on a flexible pad or sheet called a bat, then an oil-based outline was transferred from it to the piece and the piece was dusted with colour.*

BISCUIT *Term describing all ceramics that have been fired once but not glazed. Biscuit porcelain was first used by the French Sèvres factory in the mid-18th century; it was intentionally left unglazed.*

BLUE AND WHITE *The most popular colour combination used on ceramics, the Chinese were the first to apply cobalt blue as an underglaze on white porcelain.*

BRIGHT-CUT ENGRAVING *Method of engraving silver, using a double-edged tool to remove slivers of metal and burnish the cut at the same time.*

BRITANNIA STANDARD *British silverware made to a compulsory standard from 1697 to 1720. The metal contained 95.8 percent silver, which was higher than that in sterling silver at 92.5 percent. This standard was set to prevent coinage being melted down to make household silver.*

CARTOUCHE *A type of decorative border that suggests a scrolled sheet of paper. In silverware and ceramics it may resemble a shield and is often oval in shape. This border is often used to frame crests or coats of arms, inscriptions or some type of decoration.*

CELTIC STYLE *A decorative style associated with the Celts, a people who inhabited parts of Europe, including Italy, Spain and Great Britain, before the 11th century. Stylized human and animal figures and curvaceous line patterns are typical motifs of the style.*

CERAMICS *A catchall phrase for clay-based wares that are fired to make them hard. Earthenware, stoneware, porcelain, bone china and glass are all embraced by this term.*

CHAMPLEVÉ *Enamelling process in which grooves are cut into metal and filled with enamel colours.*

CHARGER *A large dish, which may be circular or oval, for serving meat at the table.*

CHASING *This technique is used for decorating metalware, particularly silver, using a hammer and blunt punch to depress or raise the surface. The metal is repositioned, leaving a design in relief.*

CHINOISERIE *European imitations of Chinese decoration and design. It should not be confused with Chinese articles exported to Europe.*

CISELÉ GILDING *Thickly applied gilding with patterns tooled in it for decorative effect.*

COMPORT *Ceramic stand with a sturdy stem and shallow dish on top, which has been used since the 18th century for serving certain types of food, such as sweetmeats.*

CREAMWARE *A cream-coloured earthenware covered by a lead glaze, which was developed in Staffordshire and improved by Wedgwood. This refined product overtook the production of delftware and was in strong competition with wares from Europe, including those from the German Meissen firm.*

CRUET *A type of small bottle originally associated with holding water and wine at church, the cruet was adapted for serving vinegar and oil at the dining table and was eventually used in sets held in a frame.*

CUT-CARD WORK *Silver decoration in which a pattern cut from a sheet of metal is soldered flat to the piece.*

DELFTWARE *A name originally for tin-glazed earthenware from the Dutch town Delft. Tin-glazed earthenware from Holland is Delftware, from Great Britain, delftware.*

DEUTSCHE BLUMEN *(German flowers) Floral decoration on ceramics based on botanical illustrations dating from the 1720s. It is found on wares from the Meissen, Worcester, Bow and Chelsea firms.*

DIAPER PATTERN *Small repeating design of geometrical shapes, such as diamonds.*

EBONIZED *A process in which a wooden item, especially one made of fruitwood, is stained black to resemble ebony. Handles on early coffee pots are often ebonized.*

ENAMEL COLOUR *Applied on top of a glaze to decorate ceramics, enamel colours are made from powdered glass and a pigmented metallic oxide, including copper, gold and manganese, suspended in an oil medium.*

ENCAUSTIC *Process by which coloured clays are inlaid in the surface of a ceramic body and baked, or a design painted in wax colours is fused to the body by heat.*

ENGRAVING *A technique for decorating metal surfaces by cutting fine lines into the material by hand.*

EN GRISAILLE *A painting technique applied to ceramics, in which shades of grey are used to imitate antique stone bas-relief.*

ENTRELAC *A decorative motif in which two bands interweave around beads.*

EPERGNE *A type of centrepiece, this elaborate silver stand has branching arms for supporting salvers or candles. It is often the most impressive item on a dining table.*

ETCHING *Acid etching, or engraving, is a method of decorating silver in which the piece* is coated with a wax, varnish or gum that resists acid, and a sharp tool is used to incise the design through the coating. The piece is then placed in acid, which removes metal in the exposed areas.

FAIENCE French term for tin-glazed earthenware, it is the equivalent of the term delftware used in Great Britain.

FAMILLE ROSE Opaque enamels in the pink family, or palette, used on Chinese porcelain from 1723. The most conspicuous colour of the pink palette is rose pink.

FAMILLE VERTE Opaque enamels in the green family, or palette, used to decorate Chinese porcelain 1661–1722. This palette was replaced by famille rose.

FAYENCE A term for tin-glazed earthenware that is used for wares from Germany and Scandinavia.

FEATHER EDGE Fine, slanting lines on creamware plates and engraved on silverware to create a decorative edge. It is often used on cutlery handles.

FEUILLE DE CHOUX From the French for "cabbage leaf", a type of decorative border typically found on porcelain pieces.

FINIAL A decorative knob of various shapes; for example the acorn finial found on the end of the handle of a 14th-century spoon.

FIRING A term applied to the process of baking ceramics in a kiln. The initial firing is known as the biscuit firing; at this stage the clay paste forms into a hard substance, such as porcelain, earthenware or stoneware. Subsequent firings then take place to fuse on a glaze or enamel colour; the number of firings depends on the type of glaze and the number of colours involved. The firing temperature depends on the material used, but varies from 800°C (1,450°F) to 1200°C (2,200°F).

FLUTING A pattern seen on silverware in which parallel grooves, which are semicircular in profile, run vertically up a column.

FRIT Powdered glass added to fine white clay to make a type of soft-paste porcelain.

GADROONING A series of interlocking convex curves, which is often used as a border on silverware. False gadrooning can be found on some European earthenware, in which the border is painted on to give a three-dimensional effect.

GILDING Applying gold to an object is known as gilding; there are several methods. On ceramics, in what is known as honey gilding, gold leaf is mixed with honey, brushed on to the ware and fired at a low temperature. An earlier process, size gilding, did not require firing, but little of this work is left today. Mercury gilding, in which ground

gold mixed with mercury was applied to either metal or ceramic wares, required firing. The mercury burned off as the piece was fired. Mercury gilding was more durable than honey gilding, but was also more toxic to the manufacturer.

GLAZE A coating based on metallic oxides, such as tin or lead, which is applied to ceramics – it often has a decorative effect. On certain materials, such as earthenware, a glaze is necessary to make the piece nonporous. The finish may be glossy or matt, translucent or opaque and smooth or textured.

GROUND Background, or base, colour.

GUILLOCHE A type of pattern consisting of intertwined ribbons, worked in either single or double bands, resulting in a series of small circles.

HALLMARK Since 1478 in Great Britain, a way of identifying the origin of a piece made of precious metal, usually silver, with official marks stamped on to the ware. Sometimes a variety of marks is used; for example, a series of marks may indicate the location, designer and manufacturer of a piece.

IMARI Japanese porcelain decorated with a distinctive look, evoked by the pattern and palette used, in particular, red, blue and gold.

KNOP Often found on top of lids or covers, a decorative knob that could be in one of innumerable shapes.

LATTICEWORK Found on silverware and ceramic pieces, such as bread baskets, a pattern in which rows of metal crisscross, forming open diamond-shaped areas.

LAUB-UND-BANDELWERK The German for "leaf and strapwork", often used to describe a decorative border surrounding a pictorial reserve.

LOZENGE Diamond-shaped decoration on ceramics and silverware.

MAIOLICA Tin-glazed earthenware made in Spain and Italy from the 13th century.

MAJOLICA Lead-glazed earthenware inspired by the strong colours of Italian maiolica wares and popular in Great Britain and the United States in the 19th century.

MONTEITH Also known as a seau crenelé, an ornamental bowl, often of silver but also in ceramic, for cooling and rinsing wine glasses. The foot of the glass is suspended from the notched or scalloped rim, while the bowl sits in iced water or crushed ice.

MOUNT Term for any metal parts applied to an item to protect it from wear.

OSIER A raised pattern on ceramics to create the effect of basketwork.

PARCEL GILDING Partial gilding of a piece of silver; for example, the inside of a salt cellar.

PATERA Circular or oval ornament decorated in low-relief.

PATINA A glowing, aged appearance imparted to metalware by years of polishing, handling and exposure to the atmosphere.

PIERCING A form of decoration in which a pattern is cut out of the clay or silver body.

PUTTO The singular for putti, which are little naked boys used as a decorative motif. It sometimes appears as a head among wings.

REEDING A type of decoration used on silverware similar to fluting, but instead of grooves, parallel convex ribs are formed.

RELIEF Decoration that protrudes from the surrounding surface. Depending on the depth of the protrusion, it may be referred to as bas, medium or high relief.

REPOUSSÉ This term is used to describe a raised design in silverware, which is created with a hammer and punch and then "pushed back" in places.

RESERVE On ceramics, a self-contained area within a pattern left blank for other decoration, such as a coat of arms, crest, scene or flowers.

SGRAFFITO A pottery technique whereby the surface of unfired slip, or liquid clay, is scratched or scored away in a design to reveal the body colour underneath.

SILVER-GILT Silver covered with a layer of gold, which often protects the ware from the corrosive effects of chemicals in certain foods.

SLIP Potter's clay reduced to a creamy consistency; it is used as a decorative coat on pottery or to stick external decoration to the body. It is also used with a mould to cast hollow shapes.

STERLING SILVER To regulate British silver, the "sterling standard" was set in the 15th century. Sterling silver is an alloy made up of 92.5 percent pure silver and 7.5 percent base metal. Most American silver is of sterling standard, but the silver content of some European pieces can be as low as 80 percent.

TAZZA A shallow basin with a wide bowl and single spreading foot or support.

TREFOIL A decorative design comprising of a flower or leaf with three lobes. A quatrofoil has four lobes.

WHITE METAL A soft base-metal alloy, which is susceptible to wear and corrosion. Sometimes this term refers to a silver below the Sterling standard which cannot, by law, carry a British hallmark.

Latticework

Patera

Guilloche

Entrelac

Acanthus

Osier

Diaper pattern

Repoussé

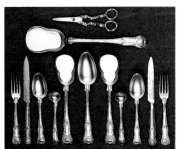

Silver gilt

PERIODS & STYLES

	16 00			16 50				17 00	
STYLE	GOTHIC (TO 1620)	BAROQUE (1620–1700)						ROCOCO (1700–60)	
GREAT BRITAIN AND IRELAND	JACOBEAN	CAROLEAN	COMMONWEALTH	RESTORATION	WILLIAM & MARY		QUEEN ANNE	EARLY GEORGIAN	
UNITED STATES		EARLY COLONIAL (TO 1700)				WILLIAM & MARY STYLE (1700–25)	QUEEN ANNE STYLE (1725–55)		
FRANCE	HENRI IV (1589–1610)	LOUIS XIII (1610–43)	LOUIS XIV (1643–1715)				RÉGENCE (1715–23)		
NORTHERN EUROPE	RENAISSANCE (TO 1650)		BAROQUE (1650–1730)					ROCOCO (1700–60)	
MEDITERRANEAN EUROPE	RENAISSANCE (TO 1650) MANNERISM (ITALY) MOORISH INFLUENCE (SPAIN)		BAROQUE (1650–1730) CHURRIQUERESQUE (SPAIN)					ROCOCO (1700–60)	
CHINA	MING DYNASTY (1368-1644)			QING DYNASTY (1644–1912)					

16 00   16 50   17 00

17|50   18|00   18|50   19|00

NEOCLASSICAL
(1760–1830)

ECLECTIC
(1830–80)

ARTS
& CRAFTS
(1880–1900)

ART
NOUVEAU
(1900–20)

ART DECO
(1920–40)

VICTORIAN

ART DECO
(1920–40)

MID-GEORGIAN

LATE GEORGIAN

REGENCY

EDWARDIAN

CHIPPENDALE
STYLE
(1755–80)

FEDERAL
(1780–1820)

EMPIRE STYLE
(1820–40)

REVIVALIST STYLES
(1830–80)

ARTS & CRAFTS
(1880–1900)

ART NOUVEAU
(1900–20)

ART DECO
(1920–40)

THIRD REPUBLIC (1871–1940)

LOUIS XV
(1723–74)

LOUIS XVI (1774–93)

DIRECTOIRE (1793–99)

EMPIRE
(1800–15)

LOUIS XVIII
(1815–24)

CHARLES X (1824–30)

LOUIS-PHILIPPE
(1830–48)

SECOND
EMPIRE
(1848–71)
NAPOLEON
III

ART NOUVEAU
(1900–20)

ART DECO
(1920–40)

JUGENDSTIL (GERMANY)
(1880–1920)

NEOCLASSICAL
(1760–1800)

EMPIRE
(1799–1815)

BIEDERMEIER
(1815–48)

REVIVALE (1830–80)

BAUHAUS
(1919–33)

NEOCLASSICAL
(1760–1830)

ROMANTIC
(ECLECTIC)
(1830–80)
REVIVALIST STYLES

ARTS &
CRAFTS
STILE
LIBERTY
(1880–1900)

ART
NOUVEAU
(1900–20)

ART DECO
(1920–40)

REPUBLIC OF CHINA
(1912–49)

QING DYNASTY (1644–1912)

CERAMIC DESIGNERS & MANUFACTURERS

	16 20	16 50	17 00	17 50

GREAT BRITAIN AND IRELAND

JOSIAH WEDGWOOD (1730–95

THOMAS TOFT (DIED 1689)

THOMAS WHIELDON (1719–95

CHELSEA FACTORY (1745–70

JOHN DWIGHT OF FULHAM (c.1637–1703)

BOW FACTORY (c.1746–76

LONGTON HALL (1750–60

UNITED STATES

FRANCE

VEUVE PERRIN (c.1748–c.1795

ST CLOUD FACTORY (1664–1766)

MARSEILLES POTTERIES (LATE 17TH TO LATE 18TH CENTURIES)

STRASBOURG FACTOR

MENNECY FACTOR

NORTHERN EUROPE

JOHANN BÖTTGER (1682–1719) GERMANY

VIENNA FACTORY (1719–186

HÖCHST FACTORY

MEDITERRANEAN EUROPE

VEZZI FACTORY (1720–27) ITALY

CHINA AND JAPAN

FAMILLE VERTE PALETTE (1450–1720) CHINA

ARMORIAL WARES (c.1650–1800) CHINA

KAKIEMON PALETTE (1670–1800) JAPAN

	16 20	16 50	17 00	17 50

18 | 00   18 | 50   19 | 00   19 | 50

MOORCROFT POTTERY (1913–)

WEDGWOOD POTTERY (1759–)

SPODE FACTORY (1770–)

SHELLEY POTTERIES (1925–66)

MINTON FACTORY (1793–)

DAVENPORT FACTORY (1794–1887)

BELLEEK FACTORY (1857–)

DERBY FACTORY (1750–)

WORCESTER FACTORY (1751–)

TUCKER FACTORY (1826–38)

BENNINGTON POTTERY AND PORCELAIN (c.1845–)

GREENWOOD POTTERY CO. (1861–)

GRIFFEN, SMITH & HILL (1877–92)

ROOKWOOD POTTERY (1880–1967)

AGATHON LÉONARD (FLOURISHED 1890–c.1900)

(1721–81)

(1734–1806)

SÈVRES FACTORY (VINCENNES BEFORE 1756; 1738–)

ROZENBURG FACTORY (1883–1916) HOLLAND

VILLEROY & BOCH (1883–) GERMANY

MEISSEN FACTORY (1710–) GERMANY

AUSTRIA

(1746–96) GERMANY

BAUHAUS (SCHOOL OF DESIGN; 1919–33) GERMANY

NYMPHENBURG FACTORY (1747–) GERMANY

DOCCIA (RICHARD-GINORI) FACTORY (1737–) ITALY

BUEN RETIRO FACTORY (1759–1808) SPAIN

PIERO FORNASETTI (1913–88) ITALY

NAPLES FACTORY (1771–1820) ITALY

IMARI PALETTE (1670–) JAPAN

FAMILLE ROSE PALETTE (1720–) CHINA

18 | 00   18 | 50   19 | 00   19 | 50

SILVER DESIGNERS & MANUFACTURERS

	16 20	16 50	17 00	17 50
GREAT BRITAIN AND IRELAND			PAUL DE LAMERIE (1688–751) PAUL CRESPIN (1694–1770) JOHN CAFE (FIRST HALLMARKED 1740; D.1757) WILLIAM CRIPPS (FLOURISHED 1743–67)	
UNITED STATES		EDWARD WEBB (D.1718 AT AN OLD AGE) JOHN CONEY (1655–1722)	JOHN GODDARD (1723–85) JOB TOWNSEND (1699–1765) SIMEON COLEY (LONDON TRAINED;	
FRANCE			THOMAS GERMAIN (1675–1748) JUSTE-AURÈLE MEISSONIER (1695–1750) JACQUES ROETTIERS (1707–84) FRANÇOIS THOMAS GERMAIN	
OTHER EUROPEAN COUNTRIES		GIOVANNI GIARDINI (1646–1721) ITALY MATTHAUS BAUR II (c.1653–1728) GERMANY	CORNELIS DE HAAN (1735–88)	
TYPES OF SILVER				

18|00   18|50   19|00   19|50

MATTHEW BOULTON AND JOHN FOTHERGILL (PARTNERSHIP, 1762–82)

CHRISTOPHER DRESSER (1834–1904)

HENNELL FAMILY (FAMILY FIRM STARTED BY DAVID HENNELL, 1735–1837;

SECOND FIRM STARTED BY DAVID'S GRANDSON ROBERT, B.1769, CLOSED IN 1887)

PHILLIP RUNDELL (1743–1827)

PAUL STORR (1771–1844)

JOHN BRIDGE (FLOURISHED c.1780–1802)

JOHN EMES (IN PARTNERSHIP WITH HENRY CHAWNER, 1796–1808)

ARCHIBALD KNOX (1864–1933)

GEORGE ELKINGTON (1801–65)

CHARLES RENNIE MACKINTOSH (1868–1928)

RUNDELL, BRIDGE & RUNDELL (CROWN JEWELLERS, 1805–42)

OMAR RAMSDEN (1873–1939

JOHN C. MOORE (FLOURISHED 1832–51)

TIFFANY & CO. (1837–)

EDWARD C. MOORE (JOHN'S SON; FLOURISHED 1851–68)

c.1725–1798)

GORHAM MANUFACTURING CO. (PREVIOUSLY GORHAM & CO.; c.1852–)

PAUL REVERE (1735–1818)

WHITING MANUFACTURING CO. (c.1866–c.1905)

JEAN-BAPTISTE-CLAUDE ODIOT (1763–1850)

L'ORFÈVRERIE CHRISTOFLE (c.1839– ; FOUNDED BY

CHARLES CHRISTOFLE, 1805–63)

MARTIN-GUILLAUME BIENNAIS (1764–1843)

JEAN PUIFORÇAT (1897–1945)

(THOMAS'S SON; 1726–91)

MATHURIN MOREAU (DESIGNER FOR CHRISTOFLE; 1821–1912)

HOLLAND

GERARDUS W. VAN DOKKUM (1828–1903) HOLLAND

FRANÇOIS M. SIMONS (1750–1828) HOLLAND

WMF FIRM (1853–) GERMANY

K.L. SLUYTERMAN (1863–1931) HOLLAND

HENRY VAN DE VELDE (1863–1957) BELGIUM

GEORG JENSEN (1866–1935) SCANDINAVIA

RICHARD RIEMERSCHMID (1868–1957) GERMANY

H.A. VAN DEN EYNDE (1869–1940) HOLLAND

JOSEF HOFFMANN (1870–1956) AUSTRIA

PATRIZ HUBER (1878–1902) GERMANY

SILVER WARES (3000 BC–)

STERLING SILVER (ENGLAND, 1478–)

SHEFFIELD PLATE (1740–)

ELECTROPLATE (c.1840–)

18|00   18|50   19|00   19|50

OTHER USEFUL TERMS

EARTHENWARE Porous pottery fired at 500–800°C (900–1,500°F), which must be glazed and fired a second time to be made waterproof.

PEWTER A metal alloy containing 80 to 90 percent tin, 10 to 20 percent lead and, sometimes, a small amount of another metal such as copper or antimony.

STONEWARE A hard opaque pottery made from clay and sand or flint and fired at a high temperature of about 1,350°C (2,460°F), which makes it nonporous. Any glaze applied to the piece is for decorative purposes only.

TIN GLAZE Usually applied to earthenware, a basic lead glaze in which tin oxide is added to create an opaque white-ground glaze. Depending on the country of origin, it is referred to as maiolica, faience, fayence, Delftware (in Holland) and delftware.

CANDLESTICKS

Since there was no electricity, or gas lighting, candles in candlesticks were an important source of light at the dining table.

SILVER

Although silver was common in the 17th century, there is relatively little surviving early silver. In many countries, silver was melted down to pay for the wars that were waged during the period, for example, the English Civil War.

FORK

The fork was introduced to Great Britain after the restoration of the monarchy and, as seen here, it only had two tines.

PEWTER

This table is set with pewter, which was a metal used in many households because silver was expensive. Because pewter is a soft metal, it is easily scratched and dented.

TANKARD

The pewter tankard, as well as other pewter drinking vessels, were common in most households in the 17th century. Glassware was costly and used in only the more affluent homes since Elizabethan times. George Ravenscroft's development of lead glass in the second half of the 17th century gave the English glass industry a firmer foundation.

KNIFE

As an eating utensil, the knife has been in use since ancient times. It was not only utilized to cut food, but also to spear the food and bring it to the mouth. The knife here has a steel blade and a wooden handle. At this time, knives were often carried in a belt strapped around the owner's waist.

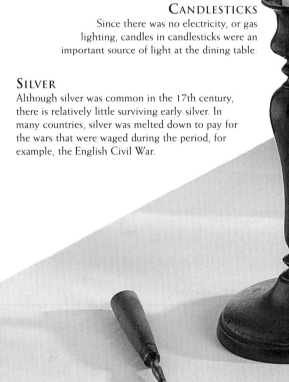

THE EARLIEST TABLEWARES: PRE-1700

The history of eating before the 16th century is not easy to trace because few artefacts have survived from then, and those that have are today mostly found in museums or private collections. It was during the 16th century that ceramics began to feature more prominently on the dining table, albeit mainly in the homes of the wealthy. Among the ceramics considered here are the maiolica wares popular in Italy and Spain, the stoneware and delftware of northern European countries and the simpler earthenwares that were common in Great Britain and the United States.

The impact of Chinese ceramics on the Western market is examined, and the resulting search for the right ingredients to manufacture hard-paste porcelain in the West is also detailed. This discovery would allow the Europeans to produce the useful and decorative wares that were so keenly sought after from the East.

This era was also a time of change: the growth in exploration into previously unknown lands led to the introduction of new foodstuffs, such as the new beverages – tea, coffee and chocolate – that eventually became so popular in the second half of the 17th century.

THE SETTING
The meal was an informal affair. Although plates were arranged symmetrically, there was no set placing for the cutlery, and the food was set on the table so that everyone could serve themselves.

BOWL
Both of the bowls holding fruit are made of pewter.

SERVING SPOON
Wood was the material typically used for making serving spoons.

PLATE
In addition to pewter plates, as shown here, wooden and delftware plates were also made at this time. This plate is being used to serve bread. The pewter plate with the fork (above, left) would have been used throughout all the courses.

SOUTHERN EUROPEAN MAIOLICA WARES

The art of producing tin-glazed earthenware was first developed by Islamic potters as early as the ninth century, when they added tin oxide to lead glaze. This created an opaque white finish to which an extra layer of coloured decoration could be added. When the Moors conquered Spain, they brought the technique with them, and from the 13th century the production of tin-glazed earthernware spread to the rest of Europe.

Examples of Hispano-Moorish pottery were exported from the Spanish island Majorca, or Mallorca, to Italy, where they soon became known as maiolica. Several Italian cities and towns became centres of production for this ceramic, including Deruta, Gubbio, Siena and Urbino.

Italian potters introduced these techniques into France in the 16th century. The French name for this type of pottery is faience, from the Italian town of Faenza, a centre of maiolica production. Faience came to be manufactured in French towns such as Lyons, Poitou (Saint-Porchaire), Nîmes and Nevers. In the 17th century, Nevers was arguably the most signifcant producer, but wares from Rouen also grew in importance, helped by the city's proximity to Paris. By the early 18th century, much of the French silver was melted down to finance Louis XIV's dynastic wars, and faience, which was freely available, became popular as a dinner ware in wealthy circles.

Since the 19th century, earlier styles of maiolica, dating from the heyday of its production in the 16th century, have been copied. Thus the style of a piece is not necessarily an indication of its date.

LARGE PORTRAIT DISH

The decorative border of this dish, made c.1530 at Deruta, Italy, is known as a quartieri. The term is used to describe a border made up of four or more separate decorative panels.

Although this dish has a hairline crack at the centre and several chips, it remains a collectable item because of the exquisite quality of the piece, its age and relatively few pieces of a similar type have survived.

The motifs of the decorative panels, which include foliage, lozenges and a scale pattern, reflect both Renaissance and Islamic influences.

The central medallion depicts a well-drawn portrait of a lady. Mythological or religious subjects were also popular. Some maiolica dishes and plates are covered completely with a single scene. This type of decoration is known as istoriato (literally, "history painting") and was a particular feature of wares made at Urbino.

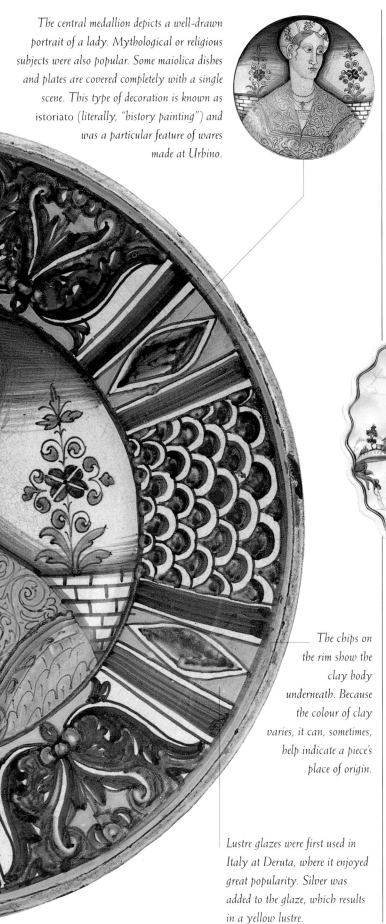

The chips on the rim show the clay body underneath. Because the colour of clay varies, it can, sometimes, help indicate a piece's place of origin.

Lustre glazes were first used in Italy at Deruta, where it enjoyed great popularity. Silver was added to the glaze, which results in a yellow lustre.

HISPANO-MORESQUE OVIFORM JAR

Dating from the 17th century, this copper-lustre jar is an example of the tin-glazed technique first introduced to Spain by the Moors nearly 400 years before. It has four handles and is decorated with bands of flowers, scrolling foliage and stencilled flower heads and was used for serving liquids, possibly wine or water. The copper lustre was created by applying copper oxides to the glazed surface and then firing the piece a second time at a lower temperature.

BLUE AND WHITE CRESPINA

The word "crespina" is used to describe a bowl or plate with a wavy or fluted rim. This c.1650 dish, made in Faenza, is supported by a foot and was possibly used for serving fruit. The central medallion, which depicts a man shooting duck, is surrounded by a landscape. The underside of the dish is moulded with shells and San Bernardino rays – an emblem adopted by the Saint, which has IHS surrounded by wavy rays.

MONTELUPO DISH

This serving dish, made at Montelupo (near Florence) c.1640, is decorated with a chequer pattern and colourful borders. It is a delightful example of the somewhat gaudy, provincial-like pieces made at Montelupo in the first half of the 17th century. Plates, jugs and dishes decorated with soldiers, horses or ladies were also made – again, strong colours were used.

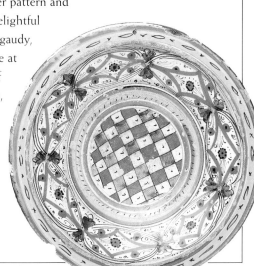

NORTHERN EUROPEAN WARES

Itinerant workers from Italy and Spain introduced tin-glazed earthenware into northern Europe. Antwerp, Rotterdam, Haarlem and The Hague were among the early important centres of production in the Netherlands, but in the 17th century Delft became the major centre. Although early pieces were influenced by Italian wares, decoration on the Delft products was dominated by motifs derived from blue and white Chinese porcelain imported by the Dutch East India Company. A style eventually evolved that combined Eastern and Western elements.

Tin-glazed earthenware was being produced in England by the last quarter of the 16th century. London, Liverpool and Bristol were among the major production centres. The English wares were also based on Chinese blue and white porcelain, although some factories made wares with polychrome decoration.

Because earthenware is porous, the body must be covered with glaze and fired to make it waterproof. Stoneware is fired at a much higher temperature, which fuses the clay and makes it nonporous; any glaze is therefore decorative. The Rhineland area of Germany was a centre of stoneware production: it had a supply of suitable clay and extensive forests – a source of fuel for firing the kilns at higher temperatures. Cologne, Sieberg and Westerwald were among the most important centres for these wares. The earliest stoneware in England, which date from the 1670s, was made by John Dwight of Fulham, who made red and white stoneware. Dutch potters who had settled in Staffordshire also made stoneware.

The Renaissance-style medallion depicts Neptune and a helmeted soldier standing on either side of a crowned sun and crescent moon emblem. It is inscribed with the initials I and E and the date 1583.

The shape of this piece is influenced by the shape of highly prized Ming wares that were beginning to be imported into Europe. It was made at Raeren in 1583 by Jan Emens.

The lid is attached to the body of the ewer with a hinge. The tab just to its right is for lifting the lid.

The body of the ewer is decorated with two "sprigged" low relief medallions that have been made separately and then attached to the main body with slip, or liquid clay, before firing.

The silver domed lid reflects a Turkish influence. It bears a Hausmarke, or maker's mark, and, like the other mounts, was probably made by a Cologne silversmith.

The neck of the ewer is decorated with a band of foliage and scrolls.

The spout is topped by a silver cap, which is dated 1585. The cap is attached by a hinge to the main body of the mount. The cap is not only decorative: it also protects the tip of the spout, which would likely be chipped if left exposed.

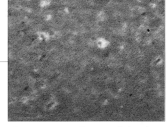

This horizontal piece was attached to the ewer to provide support for the long spout.

German potters discovered that by throwing salt into the hottest part of the kiln during the firing, they could achieve an overall textured glaze similar in appearance to orange peel. This type of glaze is known as salt glaze. The brownish glaze is typical of the stoneware produced at Raeren in this period.

At the base of the spout is a Neptune mask, which would have also been attached to the main body by slip, or liquid clay.

ENGLISH DELFT SALT

Modelled as a seated youth holding a tray in which to place salt, this English delft salt was made in London. The date 1676 can be discerned in the centre of the tray. When salt was desired, a pinch of salt – using fingers – would have been taken straight from the tray. Although predominantly decorated in blue and white, other colours have been used on this earthenware piece. When referring to English delft, a small "d" is used.

BLUE AND WHITE ENGHALSKRUG

An example of German faience, this "enghalskrug" is a jug of baluster form, with a ribbed neck. It was produced in Hanau c.1700. The earthenware body is painted with figures in a landscape and the neck is decorated with bouquets. The pewter cover is a common feature of such jugs, which were also made of stoneware.

ENGLISH SILVER SPOONS

This group of 17th-century spoons consists of (top row) three seal-top spoons and (bottom row, left to right) a puritan spoon, two trefid spoons and a slip-top spoon. Seal-top spoons, which have a flat top and a hallmark in the bowl, had been made since the 15th century. The puritan spoon is a simple undecorated type made 1649–60. Trefid spoons have three distinct points, and slip-top spoons were made without finials until the 1640s.

A FOCUS ON SALTS AND PEPPERS

The great salts of the late Middle Ages and the 16th century, which were from 20 cm (8 inches) to as much as 55 cm (22 inches) tall, give some idea of how much salt was valued.

By the 18th century the trencher salt, with its dished centre, was found in metal and ceramic. In England, by the 1740s, it was replaced by a cauldron-like salt on three feet. Salts were usually made in pairs and the inside of the bowls were often gilded to prevent corrosion. The growth of neoclassicism saw new designs, such as an oval form with a pedestal foot. Novelty shapes were also popular in the 19th century.

Pepper was normally kept in small casters. These were used in England from the late 17th century and came in sets of three – a large one for sugar and smaller ones for pepper and dry mustard. Casters were eventually incorporated into cruets, which also held oil and vinegar bottles.

Peppers

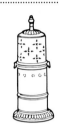
William and Mary silver pepper caster in lighthouse shape, 1694

American silver pepper caster by William Simpkins of Boston, c.1730

English vase-shaped silver pepper caster, 1775

English silver novelty pepperette, 1875

Belleek porcelain pepper, 1882–90

Stained or ebonized beech and silver pepper mill from Birmingham, 1895

English silver and cut-glass pepper mill, 1898

Art Nouveau silver pepper caster by Liberty, 1905

Edwardian reproduction style pepper caster from Chester, 1908

English silver pepper caster in traditional shape, 1919

Silver salts

Standing salt, 1542

German circular salt, c.1600

English bell salt in three sections, 1601

Trencher salt of hexagonal form, mid-17th century

German hexagonal trencher salt, c.1650

American standing salt, 1700–10

One of a set of 12 English salt cellars, 1717

One of a set of eight trencher salts by Noel Leonard of Paris, c.1720

American cauldron salt cellar, late 18th century

American salt cellar on stand, 1804

One of a set of four English salt cellars by Paul Storr, c.1811

English salt cellar made from thick-gauge silver, 1817

One of six English salt cellars in the shape of a donkey, 1840

Low salt cellar with gadrooning, 1846

One of a set of Victorian salt cellars made in England, 1852

Salt cellar in naturalism style by Robert Hennell III, 1854

Porcelain salts

Saint-Porchaire salt cellar in white clay decorated with brown scrolls and grotesques, early 16th century

Chinese blue and white trencher salt, c.1770–90

Sèvres triple salt with handles, c.1790

Belleek salt cellar, 1882–90

Hungarian trencher salt copying earlier armorial pieces, c.1890

Cruets

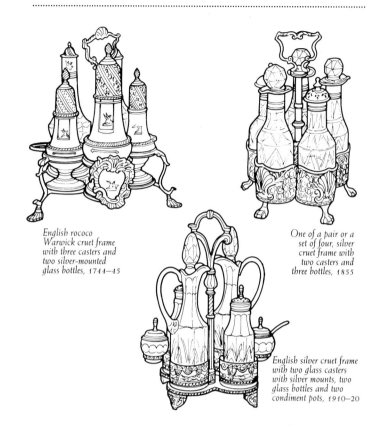

English rococo Warwick cruet frame with three casters and two silver-mounted glass bottles, 1744–45

One of a pair or a set of four, silver cruet frame with two casters and three bottles, 1855

English silver cruet frame with two glass casters with silver mounts, two glass bottles and two condiment pots, 1910–20

English salt with cut-card leaf work by Paul Crespin, 1730

English salt cellar and spoon made by Paul de Lamerie, 1734

Salt cellar in the form of a shell by the Huguenot David Hennell, 1740

French oval two-division salt cellar in the shape of a basket, 1755

American simple salt cellar by Myer Myers of New York, c.1765

Salt cellar with pierced sides and blue liner by David Hennell, 1770

Scottish salt cellar with saw-cut ornament, 1771

Canoe-shaped salt cellar by Matthew Boulton, 1775

One of a pair of English salt cellars (the other is of a woman), c.1856

One of four rococo revival salt cellars, 1863

One of a pair of duck salt cellars with spoons, 1896

A salt cellar in the shape of an elephant by Fabergé, c.1900

A silver frame with amethysts for a glass salt cellar, 1902

Art Nouveau salt cellar and spoon by Liberty, 1905

Traditional salt cellar from Birmingham, 1919

Art Deco salt cellar and spoon by Emmy Roth of the Netherlands, 1938

SLIPWARES

The concept of decorating red earthenware bodies had been around since Roman times and, in England, lead glaze came into use in the Middle Ages. A type of decoration that flourished in the 17th centuries is slipware. In this process, the body is decorated with slip, a liquid clay, before it is fired.

There were three major centres of production: Staffordshire, where the works of the Toft family were especially well-executed, as were those of Ralph Simpson; Wrotham in Kent; and north Devon, specifically in the towns of Barnstaple and Bideford. These Devon towns were particularly important, for many of their wares were shipped to the early colonial settlers in the United States. In fact, excavations at Jamestown, Virginia, have recovered a number of examples of their wares. There were a few other smaller centres in England and Wales, some of which operated into the late 19th century.

Earthenware bodies were dipped or brushed with slip that was usually a light cream colour or various shades of brown. Sometimes the decorative pattern was applied with a stiffer mixture of the slip, which was trailed, or piped, on to the surface. In north Devon, the *sgraffito* technique, in which the slip was incised away to reveal the red or brownish yellow body beneath, was used. Combing, which creates a zigzag type of pattern, and marbling were also popular. Liquid clays of different colours were used or metal oxides were added to colour the clay. The pieces were then covered with a lead glaze, often a yellow one, before being fired a second time.

The decoration was often of a commemorative nature, perhaps celebrating a royal occasion or sometimes a local event, such as a marriage or birth. Birds, animals and flowers were also popular subjects.

STAFFORDSHIRE SLIPWARE CHARGER

Ralph Simpson, whose name is inscribed at the bottom of the piece within a ribbon border, made this charger c. 1680.

Dark and light brown slip have been used to decorate the cream ground. The focus of the decoration is the central image, which depicts a stylized cat, with a detached tail, a human face and triangular ears. A mouse can be seen to the right.

The well is decorated with an interlocking pattern of diamonds and ovolo.

The cover, which was probably
used as a drinking cup, is in the
shape of an owl's head. The dark
brown eyes are set in cream
sockets. The tip of the beak has
been broken off.

The owl has a loop
handle with striped
decoration that ends
in a short tail.

OWL JUG AND COVER

*This charming red earthenware
piece was made in Staffordshire,
probably c.1700.*

The owl's claw
feet grip a socle at
the base.

The oviform body of the owl has
scrambled combed decoration in
cream and brown glazes. The
wings are tear-shaped and have
zigzag and other geometric designs
within a dot border.

The charger's rim is
decorated with stylized
flower heads and diamonds.

*Although the charger is cracked and part of the rim
shows flaking and signs of restoration, it is a very
collectable item — as is the owl jug (above), which
has also been slightly damaged over the years.*

WROTHAM SLIPWARE TYG

Multi-handled cups like this tyg were
produced at Wrotham in Kent
during the 17th century. The tyg
was used for communal drinking
and the four handles made it easier
to pass around. The handles have
rope-twist decoration and applied
studs of cream-coloured slip. The
decoration consists of three
rectangular plaques with a decorative
design below them. The plaque seen here
bears the date 1643 – the date of
manufacture – and underneath it is a stylized
roundel surrounded by studs.

SGRAFFITO-DECORATED MUG

This mug or cup was made in north
Devon in the middle of the 17th
century and was then exported
to the colonies in the United
States. It was unearthed in an
excavation at Jamestown,
Virginia, almost 300 years later
in the 20th century. The design of a
stylized flower was incised through the
slip and the difference between the
colour of the slip and the red earthenware
body below is emphasized by the lead glaze.

NORTH DEVON SLIPWARE
HARVEST JUG

The excavation at Jamestown,
Virginia, also revealed this
harvest jug. Narrow-necked
jugs, such as this one, were
used for taking liquid
refreshment out to the
harvesters in the fields.
The jug has stylized
sgraffito decoration
similar to that seen on
the mug above.

EARLY PORCELAIN

By the late 17th century, potters throughout Europe were endeavouring to discover the secret of porcelain. The faience makers in Europe tried to re-create Oriental porcelain designs on their products but were unable to overcome two difficulties: they could not produce wares that were both as thin and heat resistant; nor could they capture the brilliance of the decoration.

Many rulers collected Oriental wares and among them was Augustus the Strong, Elector of Saxony. He was often short of funds and it was this which motivated him to employ Johann Böttger, an alchemist who claimed that he could turn base metal into gold. When this project did not bear fruit, Augustus decided to turn Böttger's talents toward the making of hard-paste, or true, porcelain, and he set up a laboratory for him at a royal castle in Meissen. At first Böttger was not successful, but he did discover how to make a red stoneware. He continued to experiment and, finally, hit upon a combination of kaolin and feldspathic flux, the secret behind Chinese porcelain. By 1713 Böttger was able to start selling this new porcelain. The process was a well-guarded secret. It would be nearly 50 years before the knowledge of how to make hard-paste porcelain reached other countries, with the exception of a few factories, which had lured workers away from Meissen.

In the mid-1720s the French factory of St Cloud started making soft-paste, or artificial, porcelain by combining white clay and a frit of ground glass. Their search for hard-paste porcelain continued.

BLUE AND WHITE KRAAK-STYLE PLATES AND A BLUE AND WHITE SAUCER DISH

"Kraak" is the Dutch term, coined in the 16th century, for Chinese export wares. It derives from the word carrack – Portuguese ships that were plundered by the Dutch for their cargo of Chinese porcelain en route to Europe. These pieces were made in the Kangxi period (1662–1722).

The blues have a more violetlike tone than earlier Kraak wares, which were more greyish and dark inky-blue in colour.

The scene painted on the saucer dish depicts a scholar, mounted on a horse, followed by his attendant.

The saucer dish has the Kangxi six-character mark on its underside, which includes the emperor's name, dynasty and the period in which it was made.

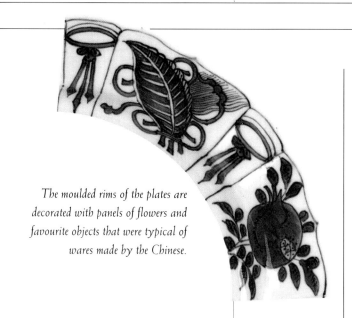

The moulded rims of the plates are decorated with panels of flowers and favourite objects that were typical of wares made by the Chinese.

The scene in the wells of the Kraak plates depicts a lady seated on a table beneath a pine tree, embroidering.

Kraak wares can be identified by the lustrous quality of both glaze and colour and the virtually translucent porcelain body. These examples clearly show why Kraak wares were so highly prized and why Western potters sought the secret of their manufacture.

BÖTTGER ARMORIAL TEAPOT

The octagonal shape of this stoneware teapot, which was made by Böttger *c.*1711, was designed by the silversmith Johann Irminger. The scroll handle and the eagle's head spout, which springs forth from a grotesque mask, are typical of the European shapes from which many early wares were derived. The teapot has a moulded coat of arms and Peter Geithner's former's mark just below the handle. The stoneware is so hard that it can be polished like a gemstone.

BÖTTGER GOLDCHINESEN TANKARD

If a blank piece failed to meet Böttger's high standards, it was sent from the factory to an outside workshop for decoration, a custom that lasted until *c.*1750. This ribbed tankard, made *c.*1720, was sent to Augsburg to Hausmaler Seuter, in whose workshop it was decorated with gilt chinoiserie scenes contained within a Laube-und-Bandelwerk border. The silver gilt mounts are attributed to Elias Adam. The tankard was most likely used for drinking beer.

VEZZI TEAPOT

The Venetian porcelain factory Vezzi was founded by the goldsmith Francesco Vezzi, who persuaded C.K. Hunger of Meissen to join him. The moulded stiff leaves on the base and shoulder of this octagonal teapot, made *c.*1725, and the colourful chinoiserie decoration of duck shooting are typical of this short-lived factory.

OTHER USEFUL TERMS

HARD-PASTE PORCELAIN (true porcelain) A non-porous white, translucent material originally made in China from kaolin (china clay) and petuntse (a feldspathic mineral). It is durable, heat-resistant and difficult to scratch.

INDIANISCHE BLUMEN Floral decoration deriving from both Japanese Kakiemon and Chinese *famille verte* porcelain and used on Meissen porcelain until c.1740.

SOFT-PASTE PORCELAIN (artificial porcelain) A type of porcelain made from a mixture of white clay and powdered glass (frit), soapstone or bone ash. It was created in an attempt to make hard-paste porcelain, but was not as strong or durable.

TEA CADDY

The rectangular caddy is of a shape commonly found in 18th-century German porcelain. The caddy spoon in front of the caddy would have been used to measure out the tea. The tea has to be tipped on to the spoon because the neck of the caddy is too narrow for the spoon to be inserted. The cover on some caddies could be used to measure the tea.

TEA AND COFFEE SERVICE

These pieces are from a Meissen tea and coffee service made c.1740–45. The decoration combines figurative scenes, based on French engravings and set within rococo cartouches, with insects and botanical studies.

THE SETTING

The table is set for tea. Because the tea caddy is decorative, it would have been on the table with the other items in the service. Tea was taken in the drawing room after dinner, and the men would join the ladies after they had finished drinking their port in the dining room.

THE ERA OF EXPERIMENTATION: 1700–1750

The early 18th century saw Chinese export tableware, including teawares, being imported on a huge scale by Western countries. Blue and white, *famille verte* and *famille rose* palettes, and armorial designs were extremely popular. Ceramics makers imitated Chinese designs in blue and white on earthenware and faience and tried to manufacture a similar hard-paste porcelain, but only the Meissen factory really succeeded at this time. Japanese patterns were also imitated and, by the middle of the century, European manufacturers were producing their own designs.

Tables were set with extensive services of plates, bowls, tureens and serving dishes, which were made either in silver, ceramic or pewter. In addition to the many dishes used during dinner, the tables were often decorated with centrepieces, figures and candlesticks or candelabras.

TEAPOT
Between c.1730 and 1770, both ceramic and silver teapots were often made in the globular or bullet shape shown here. The small size of the teapot reflects that tea was an expensive commodity.

CUP AND SAUCER
The service includes six cups and saucers for drinking tea. Tea cups at the time were usually smaller than coffee cups – an indication of the high cost of tea.

SUGAR BOWL
The circular bowl and cover were used to hold lumps of sugar.

SLOP BOWL
This large open bowl was used to hold the slops – the leftover tea leaves – from the cups before a second cup was poured.

SUGAR TONGS
Lumps of sugar were removed from the sugar bowl with sugar tongs. Most sugar tongs of the period were based on the similar design of fire tongs, which were hinged, but they are quite rare today.

TEAWARES

Merchants from the Dutch East India Company first brought tea to the West in the early 17th century. Despite its high cost it soon became a fashionable beverage and was even thought to have medicinal qualities. In England and the American colonies, tea gardens had become fashionable places to stroll and drink tea by the early 18th century.

In the home, drinking tea after dinner became a ritual. The tea was usually served by the hostess. Special wares were produced for both making and drinking tea. Because making the tea was part of the ritual, the appearance of the wares used for storing and preparing tea, such as tea caddies and kettles, was as important as the appearance of the wares for serving and drinking it.

Teapots were small in size and were made in silver or porcelain. Stoneware was also a popular material because it easily withstood the heat of boiling water. Some early teapots were shaped like Chinese wine pots. Another early style was the pear shape, which was superseded by the octagonal style. This, in turn, gave way to the globular bullet-shape of the 1720s.

Tea was drunk from small handleless porcelain bowls – cups with handles were reserved for chocolate and coffee. Chinese export examples were particularly popular and the designs were copied by the burgeoning European ceramic factories.

PAIR OF GEORGE II SILVER TEA CADDIES AND A MATCHING SUGAR BOWL

Tea was an expensive commodity and it was customary to keep it in a locked container to prevent pilfering by servants. The caddies were often housed in a fitted wooden case which was sometimes covered in silver-mounted shagreen or ivory. The caddies and sugar bowl here were made by William Cripps in London, 1750. The case is of a later date than the caddies.

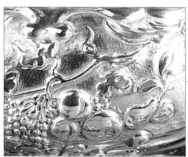

The main decorative panels of flowers and fruit are on a matt background. Many caddies were decorated with chinoiserie motifs.

Sugar bowls or boxes were often made en suite with the tea canisters.

The tea caddies have bodies with chased scrolls and panels of scalework.

Sugar nips (for sugar cubes) or spoons sometimes came with the case.

This mixing spoon was used to mix the two types of tea.

The domed lids surmounted by butterfly finials are engraved with a coat of arms.

The term "caddy" is often used when referring to a tea canister. It was derived from the Malay word kati, *which refers to a measure of weight of about 450 grams (1 pound) – the quantity in which tea was bought. Caddy did not come into common usage until the end of the 18th century. It is also used to describe the outer case in which the canisters are kept.*

Because it was customary to serve a mixture of black and green tea, caddies were usually made in pairs.

The inverted pear-shaped vase form of the caddies is typical of the rococo period.

The bases of the tea caddies are cast in the form of a sea monster emerging from the waves.

CHELSEA SPOON TRAY

Saucers were not used in England at this time, so the teaspoon would have been placed in the spoon tray. This one, made of soft-paste porcelain c.1750, has a raised anchor – the mark for Chelsea – on the reverse side. The Quail pattern here derives from Japanese Kakiemon porcelain. The tray may have been made to match a tea bowl.

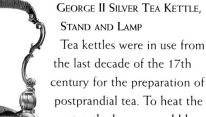

GEORGE II SILVER TEA KETTLE, STAND AND LAMP

Tea kettles were in use from the last decade of the 17th century for the preparation of postprandial tea. To heat the water, the burner would have been fueled with spirit alcohol. This kettle was made in London in 1729 by Paul de Lamerie, one of England's leading 18th-century silversmiths. The decorative motifs, which include scrolls, masks and latticework, are an early example of the move by English silversmiths toward a more ornate style.

CHINESE EXPORT TEAPOT

This teapot, made c.1750, comes from the Nanking Cargo – porcelain that was salvaged in 1985 from a Dutch ship, which sank in the South China Sea in 1751. It is painted with a design of peonies and bamboo rising from a rocky terrace. The bullet shape of the pot was a popular silver form between c.1715 and 1745 and was copied by Chinese potters for the European market.

COFFEE AND CHOCOLATE WARES

I t was not until the 17th century that coffee reached the shores of Europe and the United States, possibly from Turkey at first. The beverage soon proved to be popular and coffee houses became the ideal place in which to conduct business and meet socially. Chocolate imported from the West Indies came into favour, too, and, by the 18th century, both coffee and chocolate were drunk at breakfast by the well-to-do.

The arrival of these new beverages affected the porcelain industry. The handleless bowls used to drink tea during this period were small because tea was expensive. Larger cups and beakers with handles were made in porcelain for drinking coffee and chocolate.

In continental Europe, silver coffee pots were made with a straight handle placed at a right angle to the spout. British and American examples, however, usually had a scrolling handle on the side opposite to the spout. The spouts on coffee pots are placed high enough on the body to stand clear of any sediment at the bottom of the pot. This is not a consideration with chocolate pots, which are normally slightly smaller than those used for coffee. Because it is necessary to stir the chocolate before pouring, silver examples have a small hinged flap in the lid or a removable finial so that a molinet, or rod, can be inserted for stirring.

BAYREUTH COFFEE POT

This red stoneware coffee pot and cover was made by the German factory Bayreuth c.1725. The factory was well known for its finely potted stonewares.

Both the handle and the spout echo the geometric shape of the body.

The squared dome lid matches the shape of the coffee pot's body. It is decorated with a tasselled loop border in gilt, which is also repeated along the top of the pot, and has a cushioned finial.

The spout springs forward from a dolphin's mask and is joined to the pot by a convex bridge, which reinforces the spout.

The baluster shape of this coffee pot was found in both silver and ceramic examples. By c.1730, the angular edges that are also incorporated in this piece had disappeared.

This pot is decorated with gilt flowers. Silver lustre was also used to decorate Bayreuth stonewares.

Gilding was applied to the rim of the base. Although it is coming off in places, it does not substantially affect the value of the piece.

AMERICAN SILVER CHOCOLATE POT

*Edward Webb made this rare chocolate pot,
one of only four known examples, in
Boston in 1710.*

*The cap is removable
so that a molinet can
be inserted. Below it,
the lid is decorated
with cut-card trefoils,
which are cut from
a sheet of metal
and soldered
in place.*

*The chased fluting on the
cover and body reflect
the fact that Webb had
been trained in London –
it is a style typically
found on late 17th-
century English silver.*

*The thumbpiece,
for lifting the
lid, is in the
shape of a
divided scroll.*

*Both the rim and the foot are
decorated with gadrooning.*

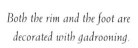

*The wooden handle is fitted into silver
sockets attached to the body of the pot.
The handles are usually of wood to
protect the user from the heat of the
chocolate, which transfers to metal.*

GEORGE I CHOCOLATE POT

The plain tapering
cylindrical form of this
pot was popular in Great
Britain until c.1730, when the
baluster shape became the
norm. By 1726, when this pot
was made, the higher dome-
shaped cover found previously
was replaced by the flatter
type seen here. The bell-
shaped finial is detachable.

A VIENNA TWO-HANDLED BEAKER AND TREMBLEUSE STAND

The Du Paquier factory made these pieces, which are decorated with
the armorials of a cardinal, c.1730. The trembleuse stand (from the
French for tremble) is a copy of contemporary silver designs. A more
common form is a saucer with a well deep enough so that the cup
cannot wobble – a design useful for the ill and those feeling under
the weather after overindulging the night before!

VINCENNES MUG AND COVER

This *grand goblet litron couvert*, or large mug and
cover, for drinking coffee shows that by the early
1750s the burgeoning Vincennes factory had
begun to challenge Meissen, which had
dominated the field until then. The
polychrome panels, painted by
Capelle (who worked at the factory
from 1746), are unusual for this
period – bird panels were normally
painted in gilt. Lids for these mugs usually
had a flower head finial – this is a rare one
more typical of a *pot à sucre à la reine* (lidded
sugar bowl).

CHINESE EXPORT WARES

The Chinese made wares specifically for the European market. Hard-paste porcelain had been made in China since the 9th century and possibly earlier, and Ming pieces were brought to Europe in the 16th century. The Portugese were the first to bring back china decorated in blue and white in significant quantities. These pieces are sometimes called Kraak porcelain, which is the Dutch derivative of the Portuguese word for a merchant ship, *carrack*.

The vogue for Chinese porcelain grew in the 17th and early 18th centuries, and tea and dinner wares were imported on a huge scale. They were more durable than the European pottery of the time and considerably less expensive. Holland and England were the main importers to the West, although other countries, including France, Sweden and the aforementioned Portugal, also traded with China.

By the late 17th century, wares coloured in the *famille verte* (green) palette were also exported; the *famille rose* (pink) colour was introduced by the 1720s. A popular form of decoration was the depiction of armorials: clients sent a copy of their coat of arms and motto to China and commissioned a service with personalized decoration. Most of these were well executed, but some mistakes were made; for example, in the spelling of the motto. Other wares were decorated with scenes *en grisaille* taken from engravings of religious and secular subjects; these are known as Jesuit wares.

Chinese potters were adept at copying European shapes. As the trade grew in the 18th century, European silver and ceramic designs were imitated. But the growth of ceramic production in Europe in the second half of the 18th century led to a decline in the fashion for export wares. In the United States, however, there was no domestic porcelain industry – export wares continued to be imported into the 19th century.

FAMILLE ROSE TOBACCO LEAF TUREENS, COVERS AND STANDS AND A LARGE DISH

These pieces were made during the reign of Emperor Qianlong (1735–95). The quality of Chinese export wares declined during this era.

The large dish, which is 46 cm (19 inches) wide, has a foliate rim and would have been used for serving meat.

The colourful, overlapping leaf design is known as the Tobacco Leaf, a popular and much copied pattern. Flowers are a focal point of the pattern; sometimes figures appear.

Along with other Chinese export wares, these pieces would have been carried at the bottom of the ship, below the waterline, while perishable goods, such as tea, were stored above.

The handles of the tureens are in the shape of pomegranate stems.

Stands were always made to match tureens.

The palette used on this beautifully rendered flower is famille rose, so called because of the strong pink colour.

FAMILLE ROSE PLATE

A European engraving provided the subject matter for the central panel of this plate of c.1735. Known as The Doctors' Visit to the Emperor, this design was originally produced by the Dutchman Cornelis Pronk. The plate's border features aquatic birds interspersed with fish cartouches.

VEGETABLE TUREEN

This tureen and cover, dating from c.1816, come from the Diana Cargo – wares excavated in 1994 from the English ship the *Diana*, which sank in 1817. The shape of the tureen was influenced by European design. The 19th-century date of the piece demonstrates the continued appreciation of Chinese export wares in the United States, where this Fitzhugh pattern was popular. It is thought to be named after the Englishman who designed it. The pattern is repeated inside the tureen.

The tureens are of pomegranate shape. As the 18th century progressed, many Chinese export tureens were based on examples sent from the West, including rococo shapes. These tureens were used to serve sauces.

The lid knobs were shaped to resemble branches.

FAMILLE ROSE ARMORIAL PLATE

The coat of arms on this rare dish belongs to the Dutch East India Company: their VOC monogram is below the lion rampant. The inscription around the edge is mislettered: it should read Concordia Resparve Crescunt, which translates as Growth Through Unity. The design of this plate is taken from a 1728 ducatoon, a silver coin used in the Dutch East Indies. The popularity of armorial wares can be gauged by the fact that there are nearly 3,000 known armorial service patterns.

EUROPEAN PLATES

The wealthy entertained on a grand scale: the number of pieces in a service is a reflection of how many people were seated at the dining table, as well as the numerous servings they enjoyed. For example, a dinner service might consist of two dozen or more soup and side plates and, because there were usually two main courses, double that number of dinner plates was often necessary. A typical dessert service included plates in addition to bowls.

As well as being made in various ceramic materials, plates were made in pewter and silver. Indeed, pewter wares were popular, and they could be found in both simple taverns and the homes of the wealthy throughout Europe and the United States. Soup and dinner plates were about 25 cm (10 inches) in diameter; dessert service plates were slightly smaller in size. The decoration on silver plates was usually confined to the shaped rim, which could be either moulded or gadrooned, and the rim was typically engraved with the armorials of the person who commissioned the service. The decorative edges of pewter wares were often derived from contemporary silver examples.

During this period many ceramic dinner services were imported from China by Great Britain. Continental factories also produced tablewares in a variety of designs. At first they copied motifs from blue and white Oriental china, but by the mid-18th century, designs included birds, flowers and hunting scenes taken from European sources, such as engravings.

GEORGE I PEWTER PLATES AND CHARGERS

These pewter wares come from a set ordered by Britain's first prime minister, Sir Robert Walpole, for his country home Houghton Hall. They were made by Thomas Ridding c.1725 and bear two stamps: THOMAS/RIDDING, which flanks a dragon, and RIDDING with an X underneath a crown.

The plates bear Walpole's family crest and the Garter motto, as can be seen on this plate.

Pewter is an alloy of tin. When first made it is silvery in colour, but with oxidization, which occurs with use, it eventually dulls to a grey before becoming increasingly dark. Pewter was made throughout the 18th century and was used extensively for plates, as well as for mugs and tankards.

Plate rims can vary. This plate, along with the rest of the service, has the plain rim fashionable from the 1720s onward. Examples with lobed edges similar to those found on silver and ceramics were also made. Plates with reeded rims date from as early as c.1710.

These chargers are 46 cm (18 inches) and 51 cm (20¼ inches) in diameter and the smaller plates are just under 25 cm (10 inches). They were part of the "Forty six dozen and half of Pewter plates" listed in the 1745 Inventory at Houghton Hall.

MEISSEN DISH FROM THE SWAN SERVICE

This dish comes from a service of over 2,000 pieces, which was commissioned by Count Bruhl, the minister in charge of the Meissen factory, to celebrate his marriage. The shell-like dish is moulded in low-relief with figures of swans among bulrushes. Similar pieces display other birds, such as cranes. The border is decorated with Bruhl's coat of arms and scattered indianische Blumen, or Indian flowers based on Oriental design, within a gilt rim.

Chargers with normal signs of wear are acceptable to collectors, but serious damage or repairs will adversely affect their value.

DUTCH DELFT ARMORIAL PLATE

Painted with the arms of G.V. Leeuwen, this plate dates from c.1750. The red, blue and gold colour combination in the centre panel was inspired by Japanese decoration and is known as Delft doré, referring to the gilded decoration. The rim is edged with green leaves, blue flower heads and seeded panels. Although Delft was in the forefront of ceramic art in the 17th century, by the mid-18th century it was being overshadowed by the growing production of European porcelain.

The charger was probably used to serve meat. Its name may come from the French charger, which means "to fill".

These plates have a plain centre; others have wrigglework decoration in the centre, in which the pattern is gouged out with a tool.

ALBISSOLA PLATES

These maiolica plates (centre and right) and dish (left), made in the 1740s, are similarly decorated with cartouches of figures, both walking and on horseback, among buildings and trees. Manganese, seen here in the sponged ground colour, has been used in the decoration of maiolica since the 15th century and is still used today.

TUREENS, SAUCE BOATS AND CRUETS

In the 18th century, it was customary for guests to serve themselves at the dining table. This meant that numerous dishes, tureens and sauce boats were required for the various courses, and these were made in both ceramic and silver.

Tureens were made to hold soups and stews – and in smaller sizes – vegetables and sauces. They were originally made with stands, although many have become separated over the years. One type of tureen known as a *pot à oille* was popular both in its native France and in other countries. The decoration of these large pieces was sometimes quite elaborate – they were often an integral element of the table setting.

Continental sauce boats usually have a double lip – one at each end of the boat – but this was a style which did not find favour in Great Britain or the United States. By the 1720s, silversmiths in these countries started producing sauce boats with a single lip at one end and a handle at the other: this design eventually became the dominant shape.

The early 18th-century term "cruet" described frames that were made to hold two bottles: one for oil, the other for vinegar. Salt was kept in its own cellar; the trencher shape of the early 18th century had been replaced by a circular form by the mid-18th century. Pepper and dry mustard or spices were kept in small casters, often found in a set of three, the largest one being used for sugar. In England, the Warwick cruet had evolved by 1750: it had a frame that could hold three casters, as well as the oil and vinegar bottles.

PAIR OF IMARI TUREENS AND COVERS

These tureens are decorated in the Japanese Imari style, which can be recognized by the subject matter, by the panels and borders and by the distinctive colour of the glaze. Although the porcelain was made in Arita, the style took its name from the Japanese port Imari, from which the wares were shipped to Europe in the late 17th and early 18th centuries.

The blue colour on Imari porcelain is known as underglaze blue, which means that it was applied before the piece was glazed and fired. The iron-red colour and gold gilding were applied after the initial firing, sometimes in several stages, since these colours had to be fired at lower temperatures.

Japanese fabric patterns provided the inspiration for Imari designs. The subject matter was typically painted within borders and panels. The tureens here include a panel with two cockerels among peonies and chrysanthemums, which is flanked by two black-lined lappets containing foliage and peonies.

Imari decoration, known in England as Japan, was often copied by European and English factories. These tureens, for example, were made by Meissen c.1735. The style of decoration was used often during the Regency period by such factories as Derby, Coalport, Spode and Mason's Ironstone.

Even though the tureens have several chips on the rim of the bases and the lids are cracked, these early pieces are still desirable items.

Figural finials are a feature often associated with wares made by Meissen. These tureens have finials modelled as hens sitting on tree stumps.

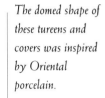

The domed shape of these tureens and covers was inspired by Oriental porcelain.

The bases of the tureens bear the blue crossed swords marks of Meissen and have Dreher's marks of an impressed quartered circle. Genuine pieces will always have painted and impressed marks.

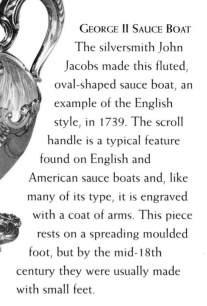

GEORGE II SAUCE BOAT

The silversmith John Jacobs made this fluted, oval-shaped sauce boat, an example of the English style, in 1739. The scroll handle is a typical feature found on English and American sauce boats and, like many of its type, it is engraved with a coat of arms. This piece rests on a spreading moulded foot, but by the mid-18th century they were usually made with small feet.

GEORGE I OIL AND VINEGAR CRUET FRAME

This is an early example of the type of cruet frame that was popular in England between 1720 and 1740. It was made by Paul de Lamerie in 1723. The design is derived from the cruets of oil and water that were used in church during Mass. Below the centre of the base is a branch sleeve, which was added at a later date so that the frame could be attached whenever desired to an epergne – a table centrepiece with a number of plates for such items as sweetmeats and fruit.

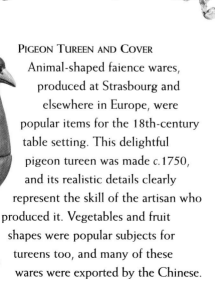

PIGEON TUREEN AND COVER

Animal-shaped faience wares, produced at Strasbourg and elsewhere in Europe, were popular items for the 18th-century table setting. This delightful pigeon tureen was made c.1750, and its realistic details clearly represent the skill of the artisan who produced it. Vegetables and fruit shapes were popular subjects for tureens too, and many of these wares were exported by the Chinese.

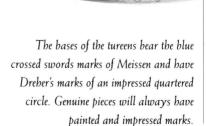

A FOCUS ON CANDLESTICKS

Most silver candlesticks and candelabras found today were made from the late 17th century onward. The height of candlesticks increased to 30 cm (12 inches) or more in the 18th century. At this time, nozzles – pans to stop wax dripping down the stem – became a feature. In the late 17th century, when candelabras first appeared, the early examples had two sconces. Three-branched candelabras were common in the late 18th century and by the 19th century five or more branches were available.

At first, candlesticks were cast in sections, then joined by soldering, which required large amounts of silver. Later candlesticks were made from rolled silver sheets, with a core of plaster of Paris and pitch. They were also made of silver substitutes and of porcelain.

Scissor-shaped candle snuffers were used for trimming the wick. Many were stored on a stand or tray.

Ceramic candlesticks and candelabras

Chinese export blue and white candlestick, c.1730

Candlestick from the Meissen factory's Swan Service, c.1739

Candelabra from the Chelsea factory, c.1765

Creamware candlestick by Wedgwood, 1779–90

Coalport candlestick decorated with naturalistic flowers, 1820–40

Minton candelabra in celadon and white glaze, c.1876

Royal Worcester candlestick, late 19th century

Silver candelabras

Two-branched French candelabra, 1709–10

Rococo candelabra from Augsburg, 1743–47

English figural three-branch candelabra, 1747

English candelabra with removable branches, 1775–76

French neoclassical candelabra, 1784

Telescopic Sheffield plate candelabra, 1800

Four-branch candelabra from Birmingham, c.1810

English candelabra centrepiece by Paul Storr, 1838

One of a pair of Russian candelabras, 1883

Russian neoclassical candelabra by Fabergé, c.1900

German Art Nouveau candelabra, c.1900

German six-branch candelabra, c.1925

Art Deco candelabra made in Copenhagen, 1936

Silver candlesticks

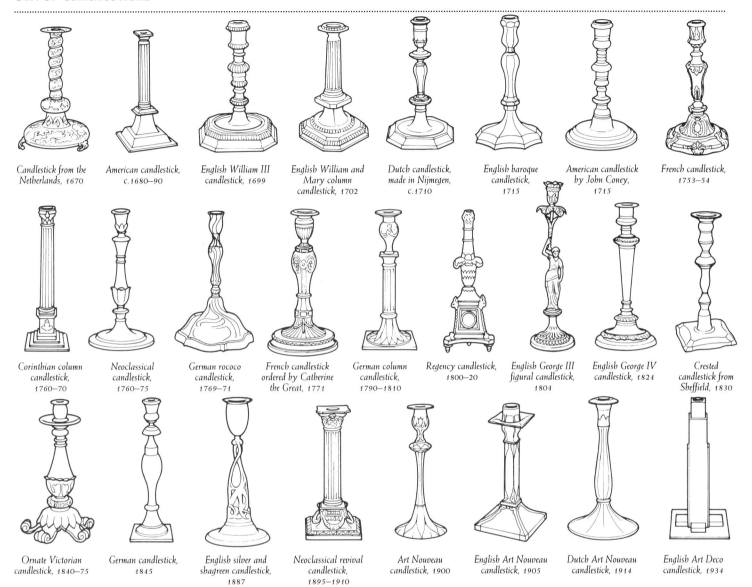

Candlestick from the
Netherlands, 1670

American candlestick,
c.1680–90

English William III
candlestick, 1699

English William and
Mary column
candlestick, 1702

Dutch candlestick,
made in Nijmegen,
c.1710

English baroque
candlestick,
1715

American candlestick
by John Coney,
1715

French candlestick,
1753–54

Corinthian column
candlestick,
1760–70

Neoclassical
candlestick,
1760–75

German rococo
candlestick,
1769–71

French candlestick
ordered by Catherine
the Great, 1771

German column
candlestick,
1790–1810

Regency candlestick,
1800–20

English George III
figural candlestick,
1804

English George IV
candlestick, 1824

Crested
candlestick from
Sheffield, 1830

Ornate Victorian
candlestick, 1840–75

German candlestick,
1845

English silver and
shagreen candlestick,
1887

Neoclassical revival
candlestick,
1895–1910

Art Nouveau
candlestick, 1900

English Art Nouveau
candlestick, 1905

Dutch Art Nouveau
candlestick, 1914

English Art Deco
candlestick, 1934

Snuffers

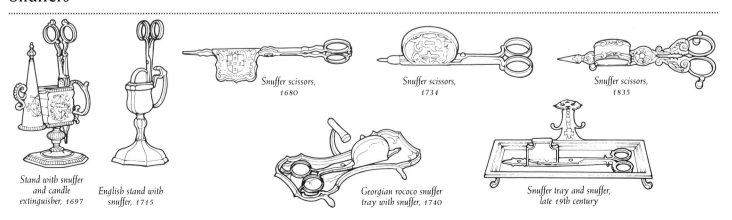

Stand with snuffer
and candle
extinguisher, 1697

English stand with
snuffer, 1715

Snuffer scissors,
1680

Snuffer scissors,
1734

Snuffer scissors,
1835

Georgian rococo snuffer
tray with snuffer, 1740

Snuffer tray and snuffer,
late 19th century

TABLE ORNAMENTS

The decorative elements of the table were almost as important as the practical ones and were often quite elaborate. One major item was the *surtout de table* – a centrepiece for the table. At first, these were made of silver and, although ornamental, served a useful purpose. They often had arms for supporting candles and some of them also incorporated salt cellars, cruets of oil and vinegar, sugar casters and, perhaps, spice boxes. In some cases, the large tureens used for serving food were designed to match the centrepiece, thus creating a harmonious visual effect. Not everyone could afford to buy these pieces in silver, so they were also made in gilded wood, faience and porcelain. By the middle of the 18th century, however, their design was such that they no longer played a functional part in the meal, but assumed instead a purely decorative role.

The table was set with candlesticks and candelabras at equally spaced intervals, with a centrepiece in the middle or with figures or baskets of flowers or fruits placed in the spaces between them. At first, the figures were made of silver or sugar, but by the mid-18th century the sugar examples were generally replaced by porcelain ones, which were often very beautiful. The subject matter, sometimes inspired by Meissen figures, ranged from depictions of mythological characters to shepherds to Chinese people.

GEORGE II SILVER EPERGNE

This is a rare example of an epergne by Paul de Lamerie and only a few by him are known. When all the components of the epergne are in place, it has four candle arms and four waiters around the central bowl.

Some elements of this epergne were made at different times. The waiters, dated 1736, were commissioned first. The centrepiece itself was made in 1737 and the feet much later, in 1846.

The epergne stands on leaf-entwined scroll and mask legs, which end in scroll feet. The feet were a later addition and made in the same style.

The central bowl is decorated with medallions of philosophers' heads set in scrolling cartouches and with two female masks.

In England, the preferred term for this centrepiece is "epergne", which comes from the French épargner (to save), because they saved people from passing around plates. The shape of the epergne is derived from the surtout de table *popular in France in the first half of the 18th century. Epergnes were first made in Great Britain c.1715.*

The candle sockets and drip pans are removable so that the arms can be used to support the waiters. The candle arms are of leaf-capped scroll and demi-figure design.

The central dish that rests on the bowl is removable so that the bowl can be used to hold fruits or flowers.

This partly fluted waiter, a small plate for serving food, has an armorial decoration matching the engraving on the central dish. Each waiter has its own branch, which can be added to the epergne as necessary; it also has three scroll feet so that it can stand on the table.

GEORGE II CANDLESTICKS

Part of a set of four, these candlesticks were made by William Gould in 1746. The partly fluted baluster stem is capped by a socket with a detachable nozzle – a feature first found on candlesticks at about this date. Their height of 23 cm (9 inches) is also an indication of the date – earlier candlesticks were shorter. The cast base is decorated with shells.

MEISSEN FIGURE

This figure of Pantalone comes from the *Commedia dell'Arte* series, which was a popular subject in 18th-century German porcelain and was copied by other factories. Made c.1743 at the Meissen factory, the figure was part of a series modelled by the renowned porcelain modeller Johann Joachim Kändler and his assistant Peter Reincke for the Duke of Weissenfels.

ITALIAN SILVER, SILVER GILT AND MALACHITE CENTREPIECE

A fine example of a late baroque piece, this centrepiece is attributed to Giovanni Giardini's workshop and was made c.1720. The central figure of Bacchus playing his pipes sits on a malachite rock, which is part of a detachable frame decorated with scrolls, shells, dolphins and goat masks – all of which are reflected in the central mirror of the plateau. The mirror, in turn, is surrounded by malachite segments contained within a decorated, shaped border standing on scroll feet. The winged putti are detachable.

OTHER USEFUL TERMS

BRITANNIA METAL A type of metal substitute that was discovered in Sheffield c.1770. It was made of a pewterlike alloy of copper, tin and antimony.

JASPERWARE A hard, smooth unglazed stoneware that could be stained blue, green, yellow, claret or black with metallic oxides. It was introduced by Josiah Wedgwood in 1774; cobalt blue jasperware is one of the trademarks of the Wedgwood factory.

PEARLWARE A form of creamware with a bluish tinge, ideal for underglaze-blue decoration. It was introduced by Wedgwood in 1779.

CANDLESTICK
An example of the emerging neoclassical style, the candlestick is of columnar form and dates from 1763.

DINNER SERVICE
These pieces are from an extensive dinner service. They are decorated with green flowers and are a fine example of French faience. The service was manufactured at the Veuve Perrin factory in Marseilles c.1750–70, and many of the shapes were copied from porcelain pieces.

GLASSES
At this time glasses were more affordable, so they were placed on the table at the right-hand side of each setting – previously they had been brought to the table when required. The glass shown is the standard shape for glasses of this period. The stem would either have been straight or have had a spiral twist. Glasses were small because wine and ale were stronger than they are today.

SERVING THE FOOD
During this period food was eaten in the French manner. This meant that for each course all the dishes were placed on the table so that the diners could serve themselves and their neighbours; any carving was usually done by the host and hostess. This meant that the food was usually lukewarm or cold by the time it was eaten.

SALT CELLAR
This silver salt cellar is one of several that would have been on the table. It has its own spoon.

SAUCE BOAT
This sauce boat is double-lipped, a style that was popular in Europe. The sauce could be poured out of either side of the boat.

SERVING DISH
This basket, one of several in the service, has pierced sides and would have been used for serving bread.

THE ERA OF CLASSICISM: 1750–1800

In the first half of the 18th century, the rococo style gradually developed out of the baroque; in the later part there was a transition from the elaborate scrolls of the rococo to the more austere yet elegant lines that were typical of neoclassicism.

In ceramics the influence of the German firm Meissen was overshadowed by the new French factory at Sèvres, which made highly decorative wares, including biscuit figures to adorn table centrepieces. During this period, Chinese export wares were still imported and their decoration continued to be copied by Western firms, but many wares were now decorated with European motifs.

The excavations at Pompeii and Herculaneum led to the introduction of classical motifs and shapes, and these soon found favour with fashionable society. The swags and garlands were particularly suited to the decoration of large pieces of silverware, such as tureens and candelabras. Classical designs were also well illustrated in ceramic wares, as the 797-piece Sèvres service made for Catherine the Great amply proves (see pp. 50–51).

THE PLACE SETTING

For each diner, a knife and fork was placed on each side of the plate, and a soup spoon would have been placed by the knife if soup was being served.

THE TABLE SETTING

When a table was set for a large number of diners, there was often more than one of most types of serving wares, such as salt cellars, sauce boats and tureens, so that the diners did not have to pass the items around the table.

TUREEN

The tureen is one of a pair in the service and would have held a meat dish such as a type of stew or soup.

PICKLE DISH

The pickle dish is made of glass and would have held a relish. A dish was placed near each place setting.

MUSTARD POT

This mustard pot and stand was made as part of the service. There would have been a spoon for serving the mustard.

ROYAL PATRONAGE

The sovereigns of many countries found that ceramic wares, including dinner services, were useful diplomatic gifts. These wares enhanced the reputation of the factory and the country that produced them. The sovereigns also bought services for their own use to impress their court and any foreign vistors. Today, many examples can be found in collections on both sides of the Atlantic.

Many of the European ceramic factories relied upon royal patronage. In some cases, such as with the Berlin and Sèvres factories, the monarch stepped in and rescued the factory from financial difficulties. Louis XV and Louis XVI even held annual sales of Sèvres porcelain in their private apartments at which the invited courtiers were expected to make purchases.

The Bird Service was the first dinner service made at the Royal Copenhagen Factory, in 1780, and is thought to have been commissioned by the Danish queen, Juliane Maria, who was one of the factory's first patrons. In England, the Worcester factory was helped through a difficult period in 1790 by an order from the Duke of Clarence for a dinner service now known as the Hope Service because each piece is decorated with an allegory of Hope. Catherine II (the Great) supported the Imperial factory in St Petersburg, as well as the Gardner factory in Moscow, which supplied the large services used at dinners for the different Imperial Orders of Knights. She also had services especially made for her by Sèvres, Wedgwood and the Copenhagen factory.

The central crowned monogram E II stands for Ekaterina II, the Russian spelling of Catherine's name, and is surrounded by a wreath of laurel and myrtle within a circular cartouche.

SÈVRES SOUP PLATE FROM THE CATHERINE II SERVICE

The service, ordered by Catherine II in 1776 and delivered in 1779, was the first neoclassical one made at the Sèvres factory. It would have been used on state occasions and included a dinner service, dessert service and a tea and coffee service, as well as a biscuit centrepiece with 91 figures. The service contained 797 pieces; this soup plate was one of 72 made in 1778.

The cameo heads, reflecting Catherine's own collection of antique carved stones, are painted en grisaille, a technique that imitates stone sculpture relief by using shades of black and white. Some of the larger items in the service incorporate cameos in relief, which were made in hard-paste porcelain and then set into the soft-paste body of the piece.

Bands of flowers are joined by gilt husks on the inner and outer rims of the border.

The gilding by this date was applied by mixing powdered gold with oil and then firing at a low temperature. A similar process was used at the Meissen factory.

The central band of the border has a turquoise ground with gold gilt scrolling foliage and flower heads. This design came from the Theatre of Marcellus in Rome.

The ground colour of the service is turquoise (bleu celeste). *The use of ground colours was found on many Sèvres wares and other colours include pink (rose Pompadour), green (vert pomme) and a darker blue (bleu lapis). Catherine had ordered the service in turquoise because it resembled the semiprecious stone; however, the colour could not be reproduced on hard-paste porcelain, so the service was made in soft-paste porcelain.*

The three reserves within the border show classical scenes and were derived from antique bas-reliefs and medallions.

MEISSEN PLATE FROM THE JAPANESE SERVICE

The shape of this plate, which was commissioned by the Prussian king Frederick the Great *c.*1762, derives from French silver ones. The centre of the plate is decorated with a long-eared boar on a mossy knoll. The spirally moulded outer border is decorated with a yellow and gold mosaic pattern while the well is bordered with *feuille de choux* (French for cabbage leaves).

POTS À JUS AND STAND FROM THE FONTAINEBLEAU SERVICE

These pieces, cups for drinking broth, come from a service originally ordered by Louis XV for use at the Palace of Fontainebleau when the court went hunting there each autumn. They are decorated with garlands of monochrome roses and gold and the stand bears the king's royal cypher. The service, originally ordered in 1756, was added to or had items replaced until 1788, the last year that Louis XVI went to the palace.

NYMPHENBURG CIRCULAR DISH

The moulded gilded rim of this dish has an octafoil shape. The blue-line and gilt rococo-scroll border encloses a well decorated with flowers, including a large spray of tulips, roses and chrysanthemums, and a butterfly. Part of the Hof, or Court, Service of the Elector of Bavaria, the dish was made by the Nymphenburg factory *c.*1762.

EUROPEAN PLATES

One major British contribution to the 18th-century dining table was cream-coloured earthenware, aptly described as creamware. English potters had been making it since before the middle of the century, but it was not until the 1760s that it took off both in England and abroad, where there was much demand for it. It was at this time that Josiah Wedgwood produced his popular version of creamware known as Queen's Ware – so called after 1765 because of Queen Charlotte's patronage.

Many fine creamware pieces were made at Leeds and other potteries outside the Staffordshire pottery district. In 1779 Wedgwood also began producing pearlware, which has a slightly bluish tinge to the glaze. Complete services were made, including elaborate centrepieces, and decoration varied from moulded or pierced shapes to hand-painted or transfer-printed motifs and scenes.

In Europe, faience makers discovered a new technique for adding coloured decoration to their wares after glazing. Until this time, they had applied the colours before firing the glaze at a high temperature, a technique known as *grand feu*. Because many colours could not withstand the high temperature, however, the range of colours was restricted. The makers found that by using enamel colours, fired in a muffle kiln (a small inner kiln) at lower temperatures, they could extend the palette of colours for decorating their wares. This process is known as *petit feu*.

A SET OF THREE BERLIN CIRCULAR DISHES

The moulded rims of these dishes are decorated with puce rosettes. Alongside the rim is a green border of a leaf-shaped pattern known as feuille de choux, which is French for cabbage leaves. It was copied from the Sèvres factory and was imitated by many factories.

A plate with a moulded rim is made by slip casting: slip, or liquid, clay is poured into a mould; after it hardens, it is removed and fired.

On the reverse side of the dishes is an underglaze blue sceptre mark, identifying the manufacturer as the Berlin factory. The factory began producing wares in 1761 and these dishes date from c.1770. Like many other European factories, it received royal patronage and it was bought by Frederick the Great in 1763.

VIENNA SHAPED DISH

The dish is realistically painted with fruits and vegetables, a popular subject matter in the 18th century. On some of these plates insects are also included. The Vienna factory made this large dish c.1770, and it bears the factory's beehive mark, as well as other impressed marks.

Using enamel colours, the plates are exquisitely painted with parrots. A popular decorative subject in the 18th century, many birds were copied from engraved plates in contemporary books.

FAIENCE PLATE

Marseilles was an important centre of production of French faience and this plate, which dates from c.1765, was made there, at the Robert factory. It is painted with a fish and bouquets of flowers. Probably the best-known Marseilles factory is Veuve Perrin; identifying a piece from this factory can be difficult, however, because many of its products have been copied over the years.

Moths and insects were also used for smaller decoration, here scattered over the pieces, and reflect the interest in nature and science that was prevalent at the time. They may hide firing damage.

FROG SERVICE PLATE

Wedgwood made this creamware plate in 1773 for Catherine II of Russia. It is part of a huge service, numbering almost 1,000 pieces. A different view of England is painted on the central panel of each piece. The rim is decorated with a pattern of a vine with leaves, which is broken by a crest with a frog. This amphibious creature represents the Grenouillère Palace in St Petersburg. The palace's name is from the French for frog, *grenouille*.

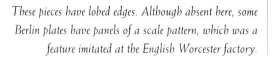

These pieces have lobed edges. Although absent here, some Berlin plates have panels of a scale pattern, which was a feature imitated at the English Worcester factory.

PORCELAIN ACCESSORIES

I n addition to plates, tureens and sauce boats, a variety of speciality items was necessary to complete any respectable dinner service. Among the items made en suite with the service were salts, mustard pots, butter dishes and a salad bowl. Sorbet cups and broth cups with stands were also made as integral parts, as were fruit dishes and cake stands. Sweetmeat dishes were typically shaped like shells, sometimes supported by reclining figures.

The 18th-century meal was usually accompanied by large amounts of alcohol, and a range of articles was used to serve it. Among the porcelain items to chill both red and white wines were wine coolers, *seaux à liqueurs* (small oval coolers that held two glass decanters separated by a removable partition) and individual glass coolers. Punch bowls and ladles were also made, since punch made with a rum or brandy base may have been drunk at mealtimes. In Great Britain and the United States, beer – along with continental wines – was a staple part of the meal and jugs in both porcelain and, for the less well-off, earthenware were common.

PAIR OF NAPLES ICE PAILS, COVERS AND LINERS

Ferdinand IV, the king of Naples and the Two Sicilies, gave these ice pails, or coolers, to his father, Charles III of Spain, as part of the Ercolanese Service, which was named after Herculaneum. The gift was not a great success because it reminded Charles of his former reign in Naples and the emergence of neoclassicism as a result of his starting the excavations of Pompeii and Herculaneum.

The moulded-relief borders on the covers were probably inspired by bronze vessels excavated at Herculaneum. The upper band has four oval reserves (areas free of moulding) painted with gilt birds and foliage set between the moulding.

The top of the lids is decorated with putti and moths.

The coolers are mounted on ormolu (gilt-metal) bases, which have pierced anthemion floral decoration and stand on ball and claw feet.

These ice pails were made c. 1781–82 at the Real Fabbrica Ferdinandea factory, the successor to the Capo Di Monte factory in Italy. Charles III moved the factory to Spain when he became king of Spain and renamed it.

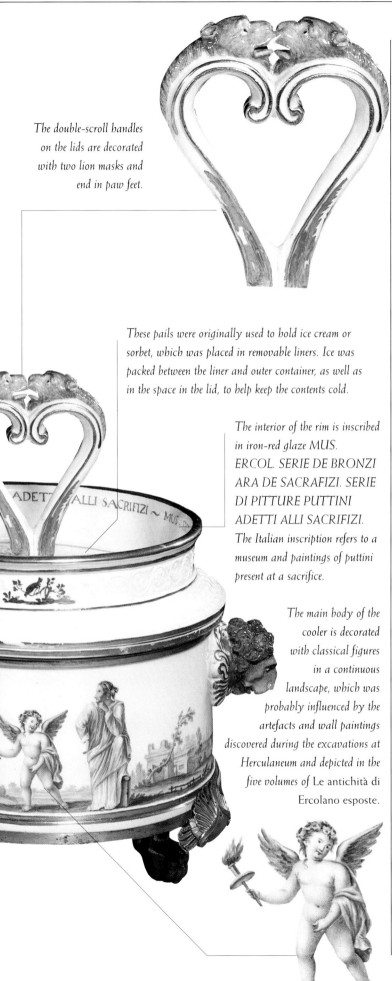

The double-scroll handles on the lids are decorated with two lion masks and end in paw feet.

These pails were originally used to hold ice cream or sorbet, which was placed in removable liners. Ice was packed between the liner and outer container, as well as in the space in the lid, to help keep the contents cold.

The interior of the rim is inscribed in iron-red glaze MUS. ERCOL. SERIE DE BRONZI ARA DE SACRAFIZI. SERIE DI PITTURE PUTTINI ADETTI ALLI SACRIFIZI. The Italian inscription refers to a museum and paintings of puttini present at a sacrifice.

The main body of the cooler is decorated with classical figures in a continuous landscape, which was probably influenced by the artefacts and wall paintings discovered during the excavations at Herculaneum and depicted in the five volumes of Le antichità di Ercolano esposte.

SEAU CRENELÉ

A cooler for wine glasses, this Spanish *seau crenelé* was made at the factory of Buen Retiro *c.*1765. With its foot supported by the wavy rim, the glass was suspended bowl-end down in the ice-filled dish. The origin of this form comes from the shape of the English silver monteith, which was also used for cooling wine glasses. The elegant garland decoration shows the beginning of a neoclassical influence.

BALTIC FAIENCE TRAY

Painted in puce monochrome, the tray, made *c.*1790, displays a scene of sailing ships near a harbour, with a town beyond. The prevalent neoclassical style can be seen not only in the flat reeded rim but also in the diaper border and the depiction of the figures, fountain and grotto.

PIERCED CIRCULAR BASKET

This basket, as its decoration suggests, would have been used for holding fruit on the dining table. The pierced sides are a typical feature of such pieces. Bow, one of the earliest English soft-paste porcelain factories, is known to have made baskets in three sizes. It made this large example, measuring 30 cm (12 inches) in diameter, *c.*1760.

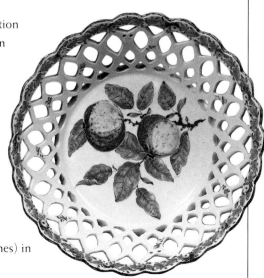

SILVER ACCESSORIES

Silver continued to play an important role in the history of dining in the second half of the 18th century. It was a highly practical material to use for tablewares, as well as a source of inspiration for potters, who often based their ceramic forms on the silversmith's products.

The types of wares achieved different levels of popularity. For example, soup tureens, already popular in continental Europe, became more widely used in England, but this was not the case in the United States. In both countries, sauce

boats fell from favour and were replaced by sauce tureens, which were usually made *en suite* with the soup tureen. One innovation was an entrée dish used to serve either cold or hot food – they were often fitted with a removable hot water stand to keep food warm. By the 1780s, trays with handles had become more common and their larger size made them more practical than salvers.

Bowls of all sizes were necessary for serving food. One type, circular in shape with lug handles and a cover and stand, was known as an *écuelle*. Used for broth, it was

originally part of the table service but by this time was used for more informal purposes such as eating in the boudoir.

By the mid-18th century, the trencher-shaped salts of earlier times had been replaced by salts, usually made in pairs, of circular or oval form and supported by feet. As the influence of neoclassicism grew, the shape changed to an oviform outline with handles and a pedestal foot, rather like a smaller version of a tureen. It was during this time that the pierced oval salt with four feet and a blue glass liner was first made.

DUTCH SILVER-GILT BASKET

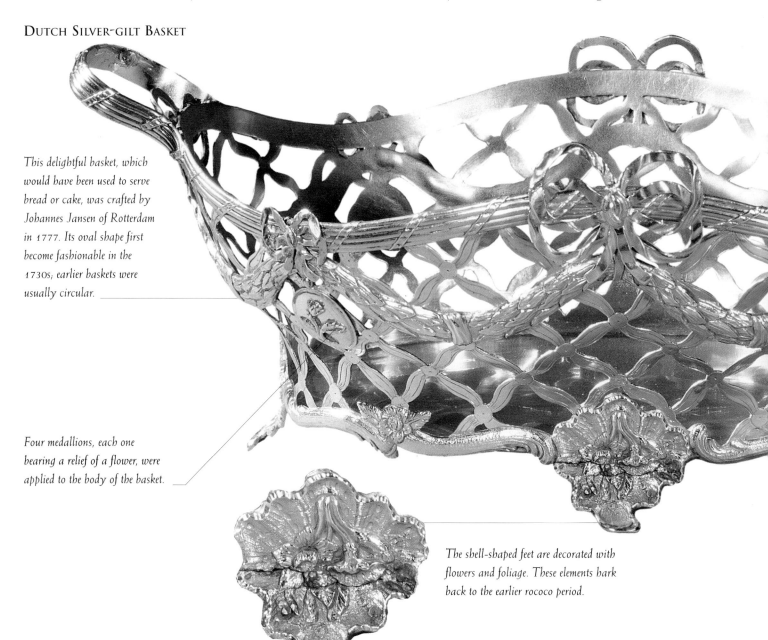

This delightful basket, which would have been used to serve bread or cake, was crafted by Johannes Jansen of Rotterdam in 1777. Its oval shape first become fashionable in the 1730s; earlier baskets were usually circular.

Four medallions, each one bearing a relief of a flower, were applied to the body of the basket.

The shell-shaped feet are decorated with flowers and foliage. These elements hark back to the earlier rococo period.

Some silver table items were gilded to protect the silver from being tarnished by certain chemicals in food. Silver gilt of this period would have been applied by fire gilding. In this process, the silver body is covered with a mixture of mercury and gold. It is then fired, which leaves a coating of gold on the object when the mercury is burned off. The gilt may disappear with wear.

GEORGE III TUREEN

One of a set of four sauce tureens, this example of English neoclassical silver was made by Thomas Heming in 1775. It has bracket handles and is decorated with bands of foliage, rosettes and plain and matted ornament. The domed cover rises to a finial in the shape of a bud and foliage. The cover and body bear the same hallmarks – matching hallmarks indicate that the cover is the original one.

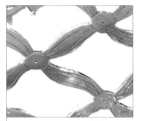

Most baskets have pierced sides: this one has a latticework design, but some were made to resemble a woven basket. By the late 18th century, repetitive decoration was done by a steam-driven fly-punch; more elaborate work was chiselled by hand.

GEORGE II COW CREAMER

This is a good example of this type of creamer, which was made by John Schuppe in 1759. The tail forms the handle and the flower decorated flap on the back is surmounted by a bee. The form was reproduced by Staffordshire potteries well into the 19th century. Beware of silver examples made after the 1760s as there are many later reproductions.

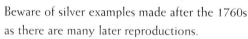

SILVER SALT CELLAR

Simeon Coley, an English silversmith, made this cauldron-shaped salt cellar in New York c.1767–69. It stands on four pad feet (most have three feet).

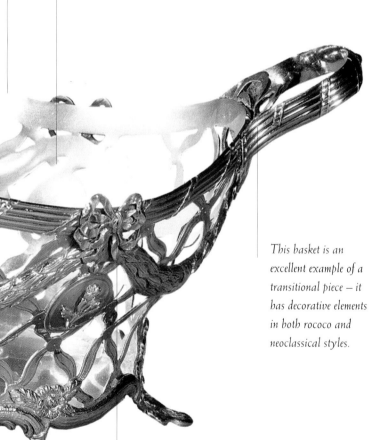

This basket is an excellent example of a transitional piece – it has decorative elements in both rococo and neoclassical styles.

GEORGE III DISH WARMER

A practical item, the dish warmer first appeared in the 1760s. This elegant piece, which has a central guilloche band and beaded borders, was both designed and made by the celebrated partnership of Matthew Boulton and John Fothergill in Birmingham in 1778. The wooden handle is detachable and the lamp, which was fuelled with spirits, is gimballed.

The bows were soldered to the body of the piece. They, along with the ribbon-tied reeded rim and handles and the foliage swags, reflect the neoclassical influence.

CUTLERY

In the 16th and early 17th centuries, people took their own spoons and knives with them when visiting friends for a meal. The fork, which came into fashion in France in the mid-17th century, was not used in Great Britain until after the Restoration of the monarchy in 1660. It is from this time, with the development of rolled sheet metal, that matching sets of knives, spoons and forks were made.

By the 18th century, it became customary for the host to have sufficient cutlery for his guests. Sets of flatware were often large and the component parts were normally ordered and made by the dozen.

The 18th century also saw the development of serving spoons and ladles as part of a composite service, because they were necessary for serving soups, stews and sauces. Other pieces included specially

designed spoons: for example, a sugar spoon with a pierced bowl for sprinkling sugar over a dessert, and spoons for partaking of tea, including one for removing tea from the caddy, a mixing spoon, and a teaspoon for stirring the tea. Bone marrow was a delicacy: to reach it, silver marrow scoops with long flat bowls were produced and some of these were made with a spoon bowl at the other end.

GEORGE III SILVER TABLE SERVICE

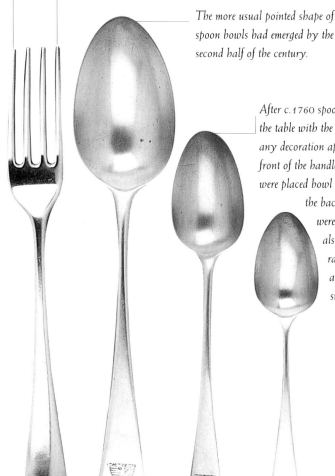

This service is a type known as composite, which means that pieces of different dates and makers were used together. This may well have been because over the years members of the same family added extra pieces to the set when they were required. The earliest pieces in this service date from 1783.

Condition is important: always look for signs of excessive wear. Early knife handles were made from sheet silver filled with pitch to give them weight. They were easily damaged, however, so the knives in most sets will be of a later manufacture.

Forks made after c.1760 usually have four tines instead of the three found on earlier examples.

These spoons and forks were made in the Old English pattern, which is determined by the shape of the handles. There are several variations on this particular pattern, which was first made in the 1760s, including Feather Edge, Old English Thread and Old English Bead.

The more usual pointed shape of spoon bowls had emerged by the second half of the century.

After c.1760 spoons were laid on the table with the bowl upward, so any decoration appears on the front of the handle. Earlier spoons were placed bowl downward, so the backs of the spoons were decorated; they also had a long raised rib known as a rat-tail to support the bowl.

The smaller knife is a cheese knife, the larger one is a dinner knife.

The forks were set on the left side of the plate, with the knives and spoons on the right, a tradition that continues today.

SERVING UTENSILS

The shaped and pierced blade of this fish server, made in 1769, is a typical feature. Sometimes the servers are shaped on one side so that the fish can be eased off the bone without cutting it.

Serving spoons were used for dishing up soup, meat and vegetables. This pair, made in 1796, is marked at the end of the handle, not near the bowl — as in the earlier fashion.

The handles of toddy ladles are usually either of silver or, as this one, whalebone. The shaped bowl of this piece, dated 1770, is inset with a half-crown coin.

A SET OF ST CLOUD PORCELAIN KNIVES

Some 18th century porcelain factories made handles for cutlery, a style sometimes copied in the 19th century too. This set of knives has octagonally shaped handles made of soft-paste porcelain and is decorated with Indian flowers and chinoiserie. The knives, contained in their original case, may have been a royal commission. The blades on such knifes are sometimes later replacements.

GEORGE III MAHOGANY CUTLERY URN

In late 18th-century England, it was customary to keep cutlery in a wooden fitted box, which stood on the sideboard in the dining room. This grand pair of cutlery urns includes a partly reeded, Old English pattern service; each urn can hold approximately 50 pieces.

Skewers, of varying lengths, were used for serving meat and game. The ring end of this example, made in 1800, is the most usual type, although other types are found.

A marrow scoop was used to extract marrow from the bones of meat served during the meal. This one was made in 1794.

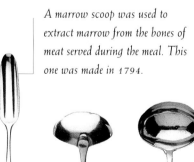

Sauce ladles are smaller versions of the ladles used with soup tureens. This pair dates from 1803 but is typical of those from the late 18th century. The rounded bowl is a normal feature.

HANOVERIAN PATTERN COMPOSITE TABLE SERVICE

The earliest pieces in the service are hallmarked for 1717. As is typical for the date, the forks have three tines and the table and dessert knives have pistol handles, so called because they resemble the grip of an 18th-century pistol. The knife and fork on the left are used for fruit.

A Focus on Cutlery

The spoon and knife are older than the fork, which only came into common usage in the mid-17th century. Matching sets of cutlery also began at that date. Although the various styles, or patterns, can be easily identified by their shape and decoration, it is important to look at the hallmarks to identify the date – most patterns are still made and many owners added to existing services as required. It is normal for old services to have new knives, in the same pattern, because they are the pieces most prone to wear. Fish knives and forks were not made until the 19th century.

The raised decoration found on 19th-century and later cutlery was achieved by die-stamping. Pieces with the pattern on both sides are "double-struck", on only the top side, "single-struck".

Serving utensils are often made en suite with the flatware services. They are collectable items in their own right.

Handles

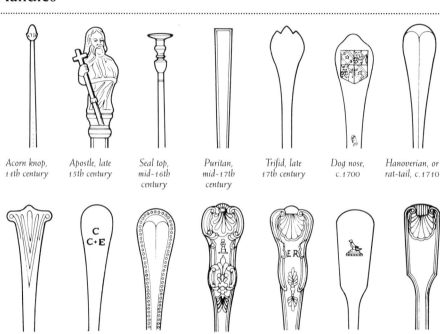

Acorn knop, 14th century *Apostle, late 15th century* *Seal top, mid-16th century* *Puritan, mid-17th century* *Trifid, late 17th century* *Dog nose, c.1700* *Hanoverian, or rat-tail, c.1710*

Onslow, c.1760 *Old English, c.1765* *Hanoverian with bead edge, c.1765* *Queen's, early 19th century* *King's, early 19th century* *Fiddle, with crest, early 19th century* *Fiddle, Thread and Shell, c.1840*

Serving utensils

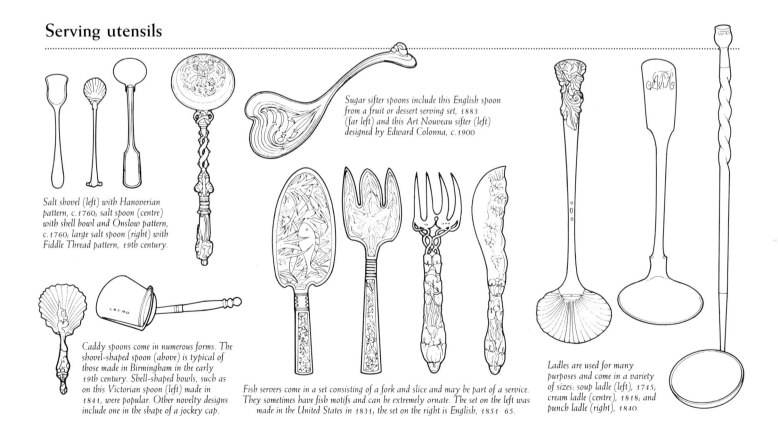

Salt shovel (left) with Hanoverian pattern, c.1760; salt spoon (centre) with shell bowl and Onslow pattern, c.1760; large salt spoon (right) with Fiddle Thread pattern, 19th century.

Sugar sifter spoons include this English spoon from a fruit or dessert serving set, 1883 (far left) and this Art Nouveau sifter (left) designed by Edward Colonna, c.1900

Caddy spoons come in numerous forms. The shovel-shaped spoon (above) is typical of those made in Birmingham in the early 19th century. Shell-shaped bowls, such as on this Victorian spoon (left) made in 1841, were popular. Other novelty designs include one in the shape of a jockey cap.

Fish servers come in a set consisting of a fork and slice and may be part of a service. They sometimes have fish motifs and can be extremely ornate. The set on the left was made in the United States in 1831, the set on the right is English, 1851–65.

Ladles are used for many purposes and come in a variety of sizes: soup ladle (left), 1745; cream ladle (centre), 1818; and punch ladle (right), 1840.

Knives

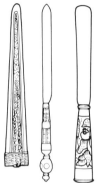

Knife with
cover, 1638

Cannon-
shaped
handle, 1698

Scimitar-
shaped blade,
1700

Dutch,
pointed blade,
1700–20

Silver-gilt
knife,
1769–70

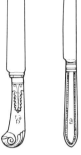

English knife,
1801

Pistol grip
handle, 1835

Finger point
blade, 1886

Art
Nouveau,
1905

Art Deco,
1926–38

Specialty knives

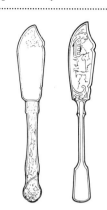

Butter knives are shorter than standard
knives and have wider blades. The butter
knife on the left was made 1826–27; the
one on the right, 1871.

Forks

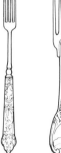

Two tines,
1660–80

Three tines,
1692–93

Dog nose,
narrow
stem, 1705

Dutch four
tines,
1700–20

French,
1766–67

Pistol grip
handle,
1775

Queen's
pattern,
1852

American
electroplated,
c.1870

Early
19th
century

Art
Nouveau,
c.1904

Pastry
fork, 1923

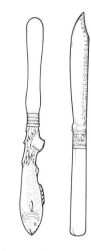

Fish knives are of a standard length with
wider blades. The fish knife on the left was
made 1874; the one on the right, 1907.

Spoons

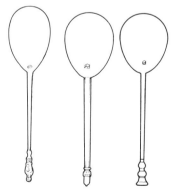

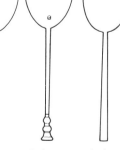

Apostle, 1562

Acorn, 1585

Seal top,
c.1664

Charles II
Puritan
spoon, 1665

Dog nose with
rat-tail bowl,
1701

Hanoverian
with round
drop, 1736

French Fiddle
and Thread,
1769–70

Spoon with
marrow scoop,
1774

Old English
feather edge,
19th century

Fiddle, Thread
and Shell,
1842

Lily pattern
dessert spoon,
1879

Art Nouveau
spoon, 1903

TABLE ORNAMENTS

The importance of table decoration during this period is perhaps best summed up by the fact that there is an example of a *surtout de table* (a table centrepiece) in Diderot's *Encyclopédie*. Many designs, in both silver and ceramic, originated in France, which led the field in decoration and fashion at the time.

The second half of the 18th century experienced a major stylistic change when fashion moved away from the curves and arbours of the rococo period and progressed to an appreciation of classical shapes. This new style, inspired by the discovery of the ancient Roman cities of Pompeii and Herculaneum, swept across Europe. These cities had been destroyed by the eruption of Mount Vesuvius in AD 79, but excavations in the early 18th century uncovered preserved buildings and other objects, which became museum pieces.

As a result, table decoration became more elaborate. Centrepieces, for example, were furnished with temples and parterres (a type of formal flower garden) made of biscuit, or unglazed, porcelain, curled paper and wood, and they were peopled with figures. Vases were sometimes adorned to reflect the latest taste for swags and garlands, medallions and other classical ornament. Some vases combined both glazed and biscuit porcelain: this style can be found on vases made for the Russian empress Catherine II (the Great). They have glazed bodies decorated with applied biscuit porcelain flowers.

A DOCUMENTARY VINCENNES WHITE HUNTING GROUP

The anatomical details in these figures, especially in the hound, show the skill of the model-maker, sculptor Jean Chabry, who was employed by the Vincennes factory from 1749 to 1777. Factories employed sculptors because the biscuit porcelain pieces look like those made of marble — one of the reasons for the popularity of these figures.

This group has a chip on the boar's hoof, the hound's tail is missing and there is a crack in the base. On the matching group, the hound has lost its rear legs and a tree stump is missing. However, although damaged, these are still very collectable items because of their early date.

One of a pair of groups, this realistically modelled
French table ornament depicts La chasse au sanglier,
or the hunt of the boar. The matching group is of La
chasse au loup, the hunt of the wolf. They may have
been copied directly from paintings by the French
artist Jean-Baptiste Oudry or from engravings of his
work. Hunting scenes such as this were also
portrayed in silver, either as figural groups or as
decorative finials on large tureens.

The group was made at the Vincennes factory, just
outside Paris, c.1752. In 1756, under the patronage
of Madame de Pompadour, the factory moved to
Sèvres. The Sèvres factory's mark on pieces is of the
royal cypher, but it was not used on the 18th-century
biscuit porcelain figures.

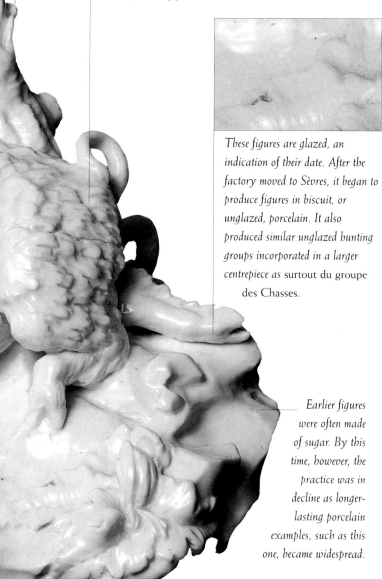

These figures are glazed, an
indication of their date. After the
factory moved to Sèvres, it began to
produce figures in biscuit, or
unglazed, porcelain. It also
produced similar unglazed hunting
groups incorporated in a larger
centrepiece as surtout du groupe
des Chasses.

Earlier figures
were often made
of sugar. By this
time, however, the
practice was in
decline as longer-
lasting porcelain
examples, such as this
one, became widespread.

PAIR OF GEORGE III SILVER TWO-LIGHT CANDELABRAS
The tapering cylindrical stem of these candelabra ends in a vase-
shaped socket, which echoes the style of candlesticks of the period.
They were made by John Schofield in London in 1795. The leaf-
capped scrolling branches end in circular drip pans and vase-shaped
sockets with detachable nozzles. The central vase-shaped finial on
some examples from this date can be removed to provide another
socket. The bases are engraved with a coat of arms; the drip pans and
nozzles bear a crest.

GEORGE III SILVER CUP AND COVER
This London-made silver cup bears
the maker's mark of John Parker
and Edward Wakelin; it was made
in 1776. The cup displays many of
the elements of neoclassical design:
it has a campana-shaped (inverted bell-
shaped) body and a domed cover and is
adorned with acanthus leaves, husk
swags, medallions and twin serpent scroll
handles, which rise from ram's
masks. Both cup and cover
are hallmarked.

HÖCHST VASE AND COVER
This outline of this porcelain urn-shaped
vase is based on a Wedgwood and Bentley
basalt vase. Here the puce and gold striped
body has moulded drapery hanging in swags
from moulded gold rings, a neoclassical
element. The classically inspired oval medallion
depicts Marsyas, Apollo and Olympus. The vase
was produced c.1780 by the German factory
Höchst, which operated from 1746 to 1796.

TEAWARES

The second half of the 18th century saw the growing use of a teacup with a handle instead of the previously popular tea bowl. As in the past, teacups were smaller than the cups used for drinking coffee and chocolate. More frequent use of a saucer with the teacup meant that the spoon tray, for holding teaspoons after they had been used, was no longer in demand.

Tea had by now become a less expensive commodity and, accordingly, teapots became larger. In the early part of this period teapots were globular or barrel-shaped; as the century progressed, however, cylindrical and oval shapes became more fashionable. Teawares were made in all types of ceramics. The United States, which did not have a home-based porcelain industry, imported Chinese export teawares as well as agate ware and other types of earthenware made by Thomas Whieldon and other Staffordshire potters.

Silver teapots were becoming more common in both England and the United States, and during this period their decoration changed from the cartouches and scrolls of the rococo style to the more restrained decoration of the neoclassical style. In the late 18th century, a form of decoration known as bright-cut engraving became popular on teapots. Festoons, husks, flowers and other motifs were gouged out with a spatula-shaped tool, which polished the silver on one side so that the design caught the light. This type of decoration was practised in the United States, Great Britain and the Scandinavian countries.

Tea caddies still had an important function in the home and numerous examples in porcelain, silver and enamel can be found. In England, the wooden tea caddy was also popular.

A SÈVRES GREEN-GROUND TEA AND CHOCOLATE PART-SERVICE

These pieces are from a service totalling 78 pieces made by the Sèvres factory in France. It was delivered to the third Duke of Richmond in 1766 and remains in the family's possession today.

As was customary, the two sugar bowls have covers. The knobs are moulded in the form of carnations and match the one on the teapot lid.

The egglike shape of the teapot is commonly found in those made by the Sèvres factory, but it is larger than normal.

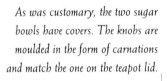

Reserves on wares made by Sèvres are usually surrounded by bands of gilding — here they include one of a foliage design.

Chocolate was drunk from the straight-sided cups, which were used with the deep straight-sided saucers.

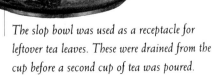

The slop bowl was used as a receptacle for leftover tea leaves. These were drained from the cup before a second cup of tea was poured.

The shape of the service's two milk jugs is unusual: it is a form that was mainly used for larger jugs. Sèvres milk jugs of this period are not usually as tall and stand on three short legs.

WORCESTER POWDER-BLUE-GROUND TRIO

Sets consisting of a coffee cup, tea cup and saucer are known as a trio; the saucer could be used with either the tea bowl or coffee cup. This trio was made by the Worcester factory c.1768 and is part of the Lord Dudley Service. The factory sometimes sent white-glazed pieces such as these to the atelier of James Giles in London for painting. The shaped panels depicting Watteauesque figures and insects within gilt cartouches are typical of his work.

The reserves on the teapot and on the rest of the service are painted with birds – a popular decorative subject – taken from George Edwards's Natural History of Birds, first published in 1743.

TEA CADDY AND COVER

The rectangular arched shape of this tea caddy is one commonly found in 18th-century porcelain. The caddy was made at the German Volkstedt factory c.1780 and is decorated with sprays of *indianische Blumen* (stylistic Indian flowers) below an iron-red C-scroll border. The knop on the cover is in the shape of an open rose.

The tea cups have curved sides and are used with the lobed saucers.

SUCRIER, COVER AND STAND

A product of the royal Bavarian factory at Nymphenburg, this sugar bowl dates from c.1770. The decoration consists of a broad black band painted with white and pink roses and green leaves. Below the band on both the bowl and stand is another banding of raised gilt triangles. The stepped cover terminates in a gilt knop.

COFFEE AND CHOCOLATE WARES

The popularity of chocolate and coffee as breakfast-time beverages continued into the late 18th century. Continental European silver coffee pots usually had a pear-shaped body supported by three legs. This design is also found in porcelain pots, but many were made in the baluster shape, which had become popular in the 1730s, and in the later cylindrical shape, inspired by neoclassicism. In England, coffee pots were also of baluster shape but, unlike those on the continent, which had a short pouring lip, they invariably had a spout. By

the end of the 18th century, English coffee pots were being made with a pouring lip instead of a spout – this form imitated the ewer of classical times. While English silver coffee pots were often decorated in the taste of the day, American examples were far simpler, with any decoration usually limited to a crest or coat of arms. One way to tell coffee pots and teapots apart is to compare their sizes: coffee pots are always larger.

European coffee cups had straight sides, and they were larger than their English

equivalent; chocolate cups, however, were bigger than both types of coffee cup.

Two variants of the coffee pot were found in England in the 1790s. The tea and coffee machine was usually made of Sheffield Plate and had a stand with a large urn for water at the centre and a smaller urn for the beverages on either side. The biggin, named after its inventor George Biggin (*d.* 1803), was cylindrical in shape and was fitted with a filter to catch the coffee grounds. Like the tea and coffee machine, it had a stand and spirit lamp.

LUDWIGSBURG TÊTE À TÊTE

A tête à tête is a tea or coffee service made with enough pieces to serve two people. It was used for more intimate occasions, rather than for formal dining. Some sets were made for only one person – this type is known as a solitaire. This tête à tête was made at the Ludwigsburg factory in Germany c.1775.

The rims are decorated with pearls in a gilt band and another band of gilt mistletoe between two solid gilt bands.

Coffee was served in the larger pot. As with some other coffee pots of the period, it has three feet. The feet on both milk and coffee pots are shaped as animal paws and have claws painted on in gilt.

An artichoke forms the finial on the cover of the circular sugar bowl.

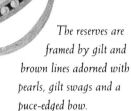

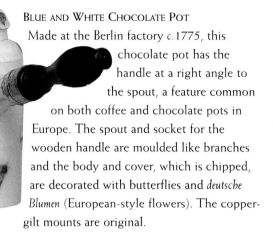

BLUE AND WHITE CHOCOLATE POT
Made at the Berlin factory *c.*1775, this chocolate pot has the handle at a right angle to the spout, a feature common on both coffee and chocolate pots in Europe. The spout and socket for the wooden handle are moulded like branches and the body and cover, which is chipped, are decorated with butterflies and *deutsche Blumen* (European-style flowers). The copper-gilt mounts are original.

The reserves are framed by gilt and brown lines adorned with pearls, gilt swags and a puce-edged bow.

All the pieces are decorated with oval reserves containing scenes showing domestic fowl and monuments in landscapes. They are painted en grisaille, a technique in which shades of black, white and grey are used to imitate antique stone bas-relief.

BRISTOL ARMORIAL COFFEE POT
Part of the Ludlow of Campden Service, this coffee pot was made *c.*1775 of hard-paste porcelain at the short-lived factory (1773–82) of Richard Champion. Its baluster shape and decoration are based on Meissen examples. The pot has an entwined branch-shaped handle and is painted with bouquets and sprays of flowers beneath a green and puce cell-and-diaper-pattern border with gilt scrolls and pendant flowers. The domed cover has similar decoration and a finial moulded in the shape of a flower bud. The family's coat of arms appears in a floral cartouche below the pouring lip.

The oval-shaped tray has lobed edges. As the largest piece it bears the most impressive reserve.

Each item, including this saucer, bears on the reverse side the blue-crowned interlaced C marks of the Ludwigsburg factory.

BELGIAN SILVER COFFEE POT
The shape of this elegant example of neoclassical silverware is typical of the silver coffee pots used in 18th-century Europe. Earlier rococo examples often had chased spiral bands around the body. Here, classical ornamentation, including guilloche and swags and medallions, has been used to decorate the body, lid and wooden handle. Like other later pots, this 1796 pot has the handle on the opposite side to the spout.

Hot milk was served in the smaller pot. As on the coffee pot, the finial is in the form of a lion with a raised paw.

The coffee cups, which were also called coffee cans, would have been used with the straight-sided saucers.

A FOCUS ON COFFEE POTS AND TEAPOTS

Tea and coffee have been popular beverages ever since they were first introduced in the 17th century, and some of the extravagantly decorated pots used for serving them reflect this. Teapots and coffee pots were made in both silver and ceramic forms and were designed in the prevailing style of the day and to reflect their owner's status.

Until the late 18th century, teapots were normally made in a small size because tea was an expensive commodity and, therefore, used sparingly. Coffee pots have always been taller than teapots, and their spouts are usually higher on the body than those found on teapots. Coffee pots made in continental Europe often have pouring lips instead of spouts. In the 19th century, the tea service as we know it today, including the teapot, hot water pot, sugar bowl and milk jug, emerged. The hot water pot was sometimes used for serving coffee.

Ceramic coffee pots

German Meissen coffee pot, 1730

English Chelsea coffee pot in classic form, with "teaplant" moulding, c.1744–49

Pear-shaped coffee pot of French manufacture, c.1770

Empire style coffee pot from Parisian Nast factory, c.1815

Art Nouveau style Meissen coffee pot, 1903

American Art Nouveau coffee pot, 1906

Coffee pot designed at the German Bauhaus school, 1921–25

Coffee pot designed by the Italian porcelain factory Richard-Ginori, 1955

Ceramic teapots

Japanese Kakiemon teapot, c.1710

Italian Vezzi teapot, 1725

Chinese blue and white teapot with European silver mounts, c.1730–40

Novelty English stoneware teapot, c.1750

Creamware teapot, mid-18th century

French soft-paste porcelain teapot by Mennecy, 1755–60

English Whieldon pineapple-shaped teapot, c.1760

English blue and white teapot with gilt, c.1790

English teapot made by Spode, 1805

American teapot in the regency style, shaped like a silver teapot, 1824–27

English Staffordshire bone china teapot, c.1830–40

Davenport Derby-shaped porcelain teapot with Japan pattern, 1870–87

English aesthetic or Japanese style teapot from the Deptford Pottery in Sunderland, c.1890

Silver coffee pots

Queen Anne tapering cylindrical coffee pot, 1709

Baluster-shaped coffee pot from Copenhagen, 1718

Baluster-shaped coffee pot by Philippe Jouque, c.1755

Spirally fluted baluster-shaped coffee pot from Augsburg, 1755–57

French baluster-shaped coffee pot by Jacques Famechon, 1771

Spirally fluted baluster-shaped Italian coffee pot, 1777

Baluster-shaped coffee pot with oval outline made by Kristiansand, 1779

Neoclassical coffee pot on square base, 1792

Neoclassical coffee pot on round base, 1806

French vase-shaped coffee pot on feet, c.1825

Baluster-shaped rococo revival coffee pot on feet, with a human figure as a finial, 1837

Art Nouveau coffee pot, 1904

American Art Deco coffee pot, 1932

Silver teapots

Agate and silver-gilt teapot from Augsburg, 1695–1706

George I octagonal teapot with engraved armorial, 1723

French provincial teapot, c.1740

Russian inverted pear-shaped teapot, c.1760

English Sheffield plate teapot, 1760–80

Dutch teapot with leaf-shaped feet and finial, 1766

American teapot with tassel motif by Paul Revere, 1796

European teapot decorated with plain horizontal bands, 1800

Regency English teapot on spreading foot by Paul Storr, 1814

George IV hexagonal English teapot, 1825

American teapot with a spreading foot and flower-bud finial, 1830

Victorian Rococo revival-style teapot, 1839

American teapot with gadrooned pedestal and shaped rim, 1840

British electroplated tea kettle with stand and burner by Dresser, 1868

American Japanese-style teapot by Tiffany, c.1877–80

Dutch teapot adorned with a simple geometric band of decoration, 1904

Austrian teapot with nonmetallic handle and finial, c.1920

OTHER USEFUL TERMS

BONE CHINA The Spode factory introduced this type of porcelain in 1794; by using a mixture of bone ash (calcium phosphate from burned animal bones) and kaolin, it created a hard, stable porcelain that was especially suited to the hot temperature of tea.

LUSTREWARE A form of metallic glaze used on bone china and earthenware to give it a glistening sheen; the most popular types were silver and copper lustre.

ORMOLU A type of bronze gilding that has a gold appearance and was applied using noxious mercury.

TRANSFER PRINT A process by which a pattern engraved on a copper plate is transferred via a tissue paper to a fired china body. It was developed in the mid-18th century and by the 19th century was a popular method for decorating ceramics.

DESSERT SERVICE

A Spode creamware dessert service is shown here. Along with the dessert plates, the service includes a sauce tureen, cover and stand (far right, bottom) and a comport (below), which would have held dry sweetmeats.

THE SETTING

After the dinner was cleared away, the table would have been set for dessert. Each place setting included a plate, knife and fork, as well as a wine glass and finger bowl.

GLASS

The glass was set on the table at the right-hand side of each place setting.

DECANTER

The decanter, which stands in a coaster, has a label around its neck to identify its contents, which could be sherry, port or wine.

SERVING SPOON

The silver-gilt spoon was used for serving ices.

TABLECLOTH

In some households, the tablecloth was removed before the dessert course, which was an indication of the end of the main courses.

THE ERA OF SOPHISTICATION & MASS PRODUCTION: 1800-1840

The classical styles of the past century continued in the early 19th century, but they soon lost their graceful elegance in favour of a stronger, more masculine style that suited the military campaigns of Europe. In Great Britain, the growth of industrial development meant that mechanical processes were introduced into the production of ceramics and there was an increase in the blue and white transfer wares made in Staffordshire. The making of bone china had become established and most English factories replaced the manufacture of hard-paste pieces with bone china because it was less expensive.

Dinner was still the main meal of the day. Although dessert services had been made in the 18th century – usually en suite with the main dinner service – colourful services were now being made especially for this course. They usually had far more elaborate decoration than that found on the plates used for the earlier courses.

The expanding middle classes liked to imitate their social betters, so this period saw the continued growth in the production of Sheffield plate, which gave the look of silver without the expense. Britannia metal and ormolu were also used as substitutes for silver.

DESSERT CUTLERY
Special flatware services were used for dessert. The dessert knife and fork shown here, which would have been used for eating fruit, have mother-of-pearl handles.

CREAM JUG
The helmet-shaped jug, used for pouring cream, is typical of the period.

FINGER BOWL
A glass finger bowl filled with warm water would have been placed at each setting so that diners could rinse their fingers during the dessert course. Although shown here out of position for clarity, the bowl would normally be placed above the cutlery on the right-hand side of the setting.

BLUE AND WHITE WARES

Chinese blue and white porcelain continued to influence the West. In England, many 18th-century factories tried to emulate it, even though their products were far more expensive than those of their Oriental counterparts. The development of transfer printing in the 1750s, however, proved to be an inexpensive method of decoration, which led to more affordable English ceramics.

To achieve a transfer print, an engraved copper plate is covered with blue ink; tissue paper is placed on the plate and the pattern is transferred to the paper, which is then applied to the biscuit body. When the body is fired, the paper burns away, leaving the design in underglaze blue on a white background. This technique was soon adopted by the Staffordshire potters. After the initial engraving on the copper plate, which could be used again and again, a biscuit piece could be quickly decorated, especially when compared with the time-consuming method of hand painting each item. Later developments in the technique allowed the use of additional colours.

By the 19th century, a whole variety of designs were produced: sporting scenes, Italianate views – including one of Rome by the Spode factory, featuring St Peter's and the Castello San Angelo – and views of England, France and the "Beauties of America". This last design was made by John and William Ridgeway and was exported to the United States. The most famous of all blue and white patterns is probably the Willow pattern (see pp.146–47), an English pastiche of Chinese patterns.

One easy way of telling if a piece has been transfer printed is to look for abrupt linear transitions from one part of the pattern to another. This will be particularly apparent on borders and on rounded objects such as cups.

BLUE AND WHITE PART DINNER SERVICE

These items are part of a service of Chinese manufacture and were made in the Qianlong period (1736–95), most probably for the English market. This type of ware inspired the European factories.

The panels, with their pagodas, willow tree and figure crossing a bridge, bear similarities to the Willow pattern, which was directly inspired by such Chinese patterns.

The trencher shape of the salts is one that was used in Europe from the beginning of the 18th century.

The octagonal dishes were used as serving dishes. The larger dishes were used for meat and fish, the smaller ones for vegetables.

As was customary at this time, the butter tub has a lid. Butter tubs often had their own stands.

The sauce boats have scalloped rims and are copied from English examples.

The borders and
scenes were painted by hand –
English examples would have been
transfer printed from the late 18th
century onward.

*The shapes of the various plates (from largest to
smallest: dinner, soup and dessert) were copied from
European silver examples.*

*This octagonal tureen, with a cover
and stand, is one of two in the service.*

DAVENPORT SAUCE TUREEN

This tureen, which was made
c.1820, is decorated with flowers
displayed in a classically
inspired urn. The flowers and
foliage are repeated in the
borders, as well as on the finials
and handles. The Davenport
factory started producing blue
and white wares c.1810.

BLUE AND WHITE JUG

Probably used for beer, this jug,
made c.1820–30, is in the
typical ewer shape of the time. It is
in the Sportsman's Inn pattern.
Two huntsmen sit outside a
country inn, with their dogs and
game birds at their feet, and there
is a country house in the
background. Note the "Wines" sign
over the door to the inn.

BLUE AND WHITE STRAINER OR DRAINER

This strainer, made
c.1820–30, once sat
on a serving dish,
in which the juices
from meat or fish
were caught. The
English landscape
scene, which was
on the dish too,
was from a
contemporary print.

DAVENPORT DISH

The idyllic scene in this dish, made
c.1840, also uses the colours
green and black, within a blue
and white border. At this
date, each colour required a
separate firing, but by 1848
it was possible to apply
three colours – blue, red
and yellow – in one firing.

TEAWARES

The influence of the French Empire style spread to factories in other countries. Jugs became helmet shaped, with tall, looped handles – a feature also found on the often highly decorated cups. Many ceramic shapes copied silver ones of the period.

At the same time, the emergence of an increasingly prosperous middle class, especially in Great Britain (which was leading the Industrial Revolution), led to a demand for the production of less expensive porcelain products. The introduction of bone china – a combination of bone ash, kaolin and china stone – by Josiah Spode provided a durable porcelain that could withstand hot liquids and had a white background suitable for decoration.

One form of decoration used on bone china and earthenware is lustre. Among the chief examples are copper lustre and silver lustre: the former required small amounts of gold oxide in its production; the latter, platinum oxide. Another type of decoration, spongeware, was produced by Staffordshire potters. As the name suggests, ground colour was sponged on to the surface of a piece, then a decorative motif, such as a peahen, a cottage or flowers, was added. It was a popular exportware to the United States, where it was known as spatterware.

A feature of the tea table was the tea urn, which was made in both silver and Sheffield plate. The vase-shaped urns of the late 18th century were replaced by a lower more globelike form. By the mid-19th century, the tea urn was replaced by the tea kettle, which re-emerged as part of the tea service. Unlike the urns, which were fixed to their stands, kettles could be removed.

The custom of having matching components – kettle, teapot, sugar bowl and milk jug – had become more fashionable. Indeed, the changes in social habits meant that by the 1850s the afternoon tea was an established ritual in the houses of the wealthy.

GEORGE III VASE-SHAPED TEA KETTLE, STAND, LAMP AND TRAY

The English silversmith John Emes made this tea kettle in 1802. Because kitchens in this period were usually not conveniently near the drawing room, the kettle was useful for keeping water hot for second cups of tea.

Hand cleaning and polishing of silver produces a bluish-silver sheen, or patina. Machine-polishing can ruin this time-created build up.

The kettle is engraved with a coat of arms, crest and earl's coronet. Silver was regarded as a symbol of wealth and many pieces were engraved with their owners' coat of arms. These are sometimes erased by later owners, which makes the piece thinner and more prone to damage at that point.

The alcohol-burning lamp was a practical device for keeping the water hot.

The circular tray, with gadrooned edges, has four ball-shaped feet and two bracket-shaped handles.

The domed lid, with its ivory bun-shaped finial, is removable.

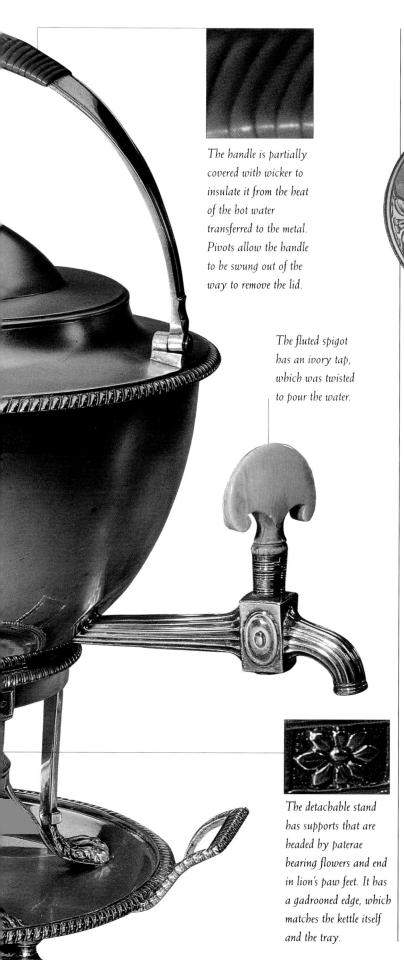

The handle is partially covered with wicker to insulate it from the heat of the hot water transferred to the metal. Pivots allow the handle to be swung out of the way to remove the lid.

The fluted spigot has an ivory tap, which was twisted to pour the water.

The detachable stand has supports that are headed by paterae bearing flowers and end in lion's paw feet. It has a gadrooned edge, which matches the kettle itself and the tray.

TEACUP AND SAUCER

This English example was made at the Miles Mason factory c.1810. Its neoclassically inspired decoration includes gilded panels and scenes *en grisaille*. These scenes are an example of bat printing, which is similar to transfer printing but the design is transferred on to the piece in oil using a bat (a flexible sheet) of gelatine or glue, hence the name. Because there is no paper, the result is a finer print.

VIENNA BLUE-GROUND TEACUP AND SAUCER

Made in 1801, the cup is of campana form and has a swan's head handle. The blue ground is decorated with gilt swags and acanthus leaves within a gilt band. The outer white banding has gilded cartouches and stylized foliage. Some cups of this Empire form are decorated with panels depicting famous people, old master paintings or flowers and foliage.

A HARLEY LUSTRE TEAPOT AND COVER

The shape of this bone china teapot, made c.1810–25, copies the silver shapes prevalent at the time. Some have overall silver lustre decoration that imitated real silver, which may have been too expensive for the owners. The pleasing decoration features, in addition to an overall pattern of silver leaves, flowers in red and blue and a central panel of flowers highlighted in iron red.

DESSERT SERVICES

Many factories made dessert services as part of a large dinner service and the total number of pieces in these combined sets could be as many as 500. Dessert services included comports, fruit stands, dishes, sauce tureens, ice-cream or custard cups, wine coolers, and ice-cream or fruit coolers, although not all of these components are found in services made in Great Britain. The table was cleared after the main courses, and in some English households the cloth was removed, and the dessert service would then be laid.

Special services of cutlery were produced for dessert and these were often made in silver-gilt. Sometimes the handles were chased with such designs as vine leaves with fruit – an appropriate decoration for this part of the meal.

Fruit dishes and stands were also made in silver and silver-gilt and, indeed, some of the shapes and moulded decoration of porcelain dishes were directly inspired by their silver counterparts. The painted decoration was of a high quality and made use of ground colours, gilding and painted panels – often floral – to produce sumptuous sets.

French porcelain continued to play an influential role in design and many of the dessert services made in the numerous small individual Parisian factories were exported abroad and even sold in the retailer Phillips's London saleroom. Some Empire design services feature porcelain openwork baskets supported by winged figures – one example can be seen in the White House. The American porcelain industry did not really start until the launch of the Tucker factory in Philadelphia in 1827, so ceramics were still imported. President Monroe, for example, used a French green-ground dessert service which he bought in Paris between 1802 and 1807.

DERBY DESSERT SERVICE

The service bears the crown, crossed batons and D mark, as well as the pattern number 311, in blue on the underside of individual pieces. This indicates that the service was made c.1800, during the Duesbury and Kean partnership.

The leaf shape of some of the dishes is an enduring feature of Derby services.

The yellow ground colour is quite a rare colour, since yellow is very difficult to achieve consistently in firing.

The navette shape of the sauce tureens and stands was a popular neoclassical shape.

The painted flowers are all botanical specimens, and their Latin and English names are recorded on the reverse of each piece. Although it is sometimes possible to identify the artist from the factory's records, in this case only an attribution can be made – to John Brewer, who was a flower painter working at the factory at this period.

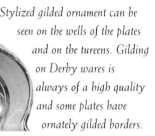

CHAMBERLAIN'S WORCESTER DESSERT SERVICE

This service, made c.1815, shows how colourful some of the English Regency services can be. The decoration, apart from a gilt band of foliage around the wells, is all found on the lilac ground borders, which have painted reserves of specimen flowers. The two-handled centre dish stands on a foot, as is customary. The vase-shaped pieces – one with a cover and the other without – are sauce tureens.

Stylized gilded ornament can be seen on the wells of the plates and on the tureens. Gilding on Derby wares is always of a high quality and some plates have ornately gilded borders.

PARIS PART DESSERT SERVICE

Made at the La Courtille factory c.1805, these dessert components are from a dinner and dessert service containing 220 different items. The square fruit dish and custard cup and cover are decorated in black and gold. The dish has a central flower-head medallion and both have designs incorporating swans, urns and trailing foliage, motifs popular in France.

GEORGE III SILVER-GILT DESSERT SERVICE

Hallmarked for 1818 and 1819, the service was made by Paul Storr and includes ice spoons, sifting spoons and grape scissors, as well as dessert spoons, forks, knives and cheese knives. The shape of the handles are in the Hourglass pattern. British silversmiths adopted it from the French in the early 19th century. Originally there were 24 place settings but another 12 were added in 1849.

ACCESSORIES

By the beginning of the 19th century, there was a move away from the light elegance that was preferred in the late 18th century toward a more robust style. This change was at first influenced by the designs of ancient Greece, but soon Roman classicism had become dominant, perhaps because it was more suited to the martial victories of Napoleon. His conquest of Egypt also influenced fashionable taste, but by the time of his final defeat at Waterloo, there were signs of a rococo revival emerging. All these differing influences can be seen in both silver and ceramic objects of the period – as they had done in the past, most countries looked to France for inspiration.

Dining tables were still adorned with many different objects necessary for eating, and in Great Britain several new forms were introduced. One practical one was the argyle – a gravy pot with a spout – named after the Scottish Duke of Argyll. It had an inner lining in which hot water could be poured to help keep the gravy warm. The spout was normally set low on the pot so that when the gravy was poured, the fat – which would have risen to the top – was left behind.

Circular and oval, domed silver or Sheffield plate dish covers came into more common usage in an attempt to keep food hot. The chafing dish – a small charcoal brazier and stand – was still used to keep plates warm and for the preparation of food at the table. Circular butter dishes, with lids and stands, were by now being made in both ceramic and silver, replacing the shell-shaped dishes used earlier in the 18th century. One delightful item at this time was the silver honey pot made to resemble the straw skeps used in bee-keeping, with a cover surmounted by a bee finial.

GEORGE III OVAL EGG CRUET

The cruet frame and egg cups were made in 1809 by Paul Storr, a leading Regency silversmith.

The central handle is in the neoclassically inspired reed and tie form ending in a bud finial.

The circular frame has foliage feet and six Mercury staff supports. The edge is decorated with an entrelac pattern.

Some circular stands were designed so that they could revolve.

GEORGE III BUTTER DISHES

Lion's paws and scroll feet are often used by the maker of these butter dishes, Paul Storr, who made them in 1809. The dishes have cast and chased banded decoration of arcading and anthemion ornament. The butter would have been placed in the plain glass liner.

The rims and sides of the egg cups have bands of fluting.

The egg cups, which were made in a fluted vase form, have gilded interiors to combat possible corrosion caused by eggs and salt.

The spoons are supported by rings attached to the stand.

The six egg spoons are of the Fiddle, Thread and Shell pattern, and their handles are engraved with a crest. The spoons were made 20 years after the cruet, in 1829, and by a different maker.

NYMPHENBURG OVAL TRAY

This gold-ground tray, made in 1813, followed the French fashion of the time, which was brought to the Nymphenburg factory by J.G. Meyerhuber, who worked there from 1812 to 1815. He signed the painted reserve, which depicts lions in a jungle clearing. The tray has an impressed shield mark, with the letter L, and an incised W beneath.

GEORGE III OVAL SOUP TUREEN AND STAND

Made by Paul Storr in 1819, this tureen shows the different decorative elements found in Regency silver, such as the gadrooning on the borders. The feet on the stand are of scroll and lion's paw form, but those on the tureen are scrolls and shells. The cover has a removable handle.

A Focus on 19th-century Motifs

The 19th century began by following the lighter neoclassical taste of the previous century but soon developed into the heavier Empire style, which reflected the political events of the time. A variety of styles, including Gothic and rococo, emerged, and motifs from these styles were incorporated into the designs of the period. By the mid-19th century, these styles were joined by naturalism, and neoclassicism continued to have an influence. Many items were made in a hybrid of styles, and such excesses led "reformers" to make wares that were true to the style they copied. A new style, Art Nouveau, emerged at the end of the century.

Ceramic wares

Japanese revival dessert plate in an Imari style, by Derby factory, c.1800

Neoclassical centrepiece, with biscuit figures and bronze mounts, commissioned for the Russian court, c.1802

Chinoiserie bone china cup with cover and saucer, decorated with the Chinese Sports pattern, 1805–10

Bowl by Spode factory decorated in the Regency revival of chinoiserie, c.1810

Classical porcelain pedestal vase and cover, made by Worcester, c.1813–40

Porcelain dish, with a central panel of birds, in the 18th-century revival style, made at Worcester, c.1820

Worcester dessert plate, with flowers in reserves, in the 18th-century French revival style, made c.1825

Rockingham cup and saucer, with overlapping leaves, in rococo revival style, made 1826–30

Two-branch candelabra in the rococo revival style by the Meissen factory, 1840

Sugar bowl from a rococo revival tea service made at the Schlaggenwald factory, 1841

English Gothic revival milk jug produced by Charles Meigh, 1842

German coffee pot in the Renaissance revival style, c.1850–80

Chinoiserie bone china plate produced by Royal Worcester, c.1860–70

Renaissance revival milk jug by Bing & Grøndahl of Copenhagen, c.1860

Belleek table centrepiece in the naturalistic form of a lily flower and leaves, 1869

A centrepiece with women by Copeland in a mixture of rococo and classical revival styles, c.1870

Candelabra made in Staffordshire by Minton in rococo and classical styles, c.1870

Rococo revival centrepiece from the French Pouyat factory, 1878

Teapot by the Hammersley firm in the Regency revival style, c.1890

Silver wares

English tea urn by Digby
Scott and Benjamin Smith in
the classical revival style, 1806

English candlestick in the
rococo style, 1809

Cup and saucer in the
neoclassical style used at the
Tuileries, 1810

Neoclassical wine cooler made
in England by Rundell, Bridge
& Rundell, 1810

French neoclassical coffee pot
bearing the arms of
Napoleon I, c.1810

Birmingham candlestick in the
neoclassical style, made by
Matthew Boulton, 1813

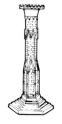

Gothic candlestick in the form
of a stone tower, by William
Elliott of London, 1814

American sauce boat in the
French neoclassical style,
c.1815

Rococo revival dessert cutlery
with baccanalian figures, by
Edward C. Farrell, 1816–18

Neoclassical soup tureen on a
pedestal by Jean-Baptiste-
Claude Odiot, 1817

Candlestick by Samuel
Whitford in rococo revival
and chinoiserie styles, 1819

English wine cup by William
Bateman in Gothic and rococo
revival styles, 1836

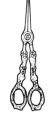

English candlestick in rococo
revival style by Benjamin
Smith, 1836

Melon pattern coffee pot in
rococo revival style, c.1840

Neoclassical teapot made in
The Hague, 1840

English grape scissors of
naturalistic form, 1842

Gothic candlestick, 1843

Engraved sugar bowl in
a 17th-century revival
style, c.1845

Rococo revival milk jug
with a Louis XV pattern,
c.1845–60

American kettle and stand in
the rococo revival style, by
John Chandler Moore, 1850

Punch ladle with a plant-
like handle in the
naturalistic form, 1853

American coffee pot in the
Gothic revival style by
Joseph Angell, 1854–55

German wine cooler in the
rococo revival style by
Hermann Julius Wilm, c.1855

English teapot in the rococo
revival style by James Dixon
& Sons, 1866–67

Japanese-inspired salver in
the Aesthetic Movement style,
made in Birmingham, 1879

Candlestick in the
neoclassical style, c.1880

American jug in the Aesthetic
Movement style, by Theodore
B. Starr, c.1885

American tea kettle and stand in
the colonial revival style, by
Black, Starr & Frost, c.1885

American vase in a combination
of naturalistic and Art
Nouveau styles, 1893

Vegetable dish by André Aucoc
in the rococo revival style,
c.1900

TABLE CENTREPIECES

The popularity of table centrepieces did not diminish in the early 19th century and, indeed, the widespread adoption of the Empire style contributed to their continuation. Designs were very much influenced by Roman and Egyptian motifs, and ornaments included vases, columns and figures based on antique examples. They were still designed to extend along the length of the table and, for a very grand household, could measure as much as 10 m (33 feet) in length.

Although elaborate porcelain constructions were still made, the mirrored plateau was a popular form. A silver plate or stand, it usually had D-shaped ends and was supported on feet – the mirror surface was enclosed by low pierced sides. Some of these had a removable middle section so that the size could be adjusted – much like some dining tables of the period. Candelabras and baskets, often supported by figures, were placed on the reflective surface. A French gilt-bronze example is regularly used in the White House in Washington, and there is also a rare American silver example in their collection.

The epergne was an 18th century form that continued to flourish throughout the 19th century. Cups and covers were still made too. In Great Britain, large silver and silver-gilt tankards were made as presentation pieces and, with sideboard dishes, were part of the display silver found in the dining room. The number of branches on candelabras increased from the usual two or three of the late 18th century to four or more, and candelabras became more elaborate as the period progressed.

GEORGE III SEVEN-LIGHT CANDELABRA CENTREPIECE

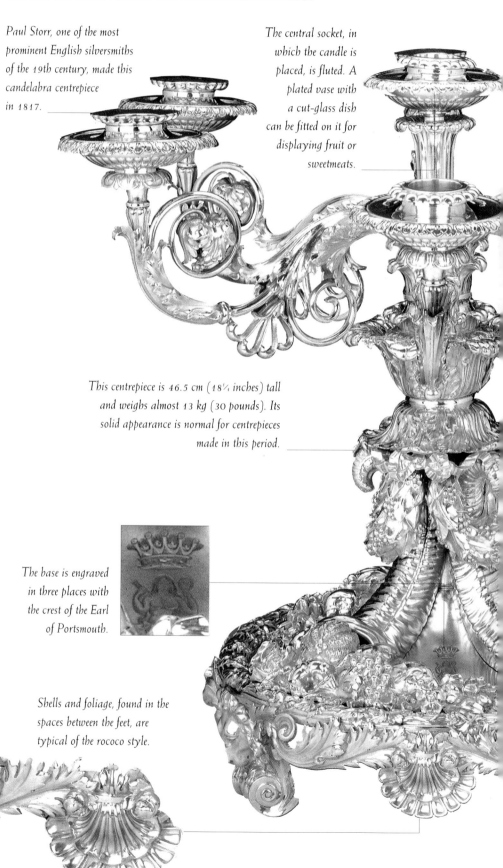

Paul Storr, one of the most prominent English silversmiths of the 19th century, made this candelabra centrepiece in 1817.

The central socket, in which the candle is placed, is fluted. A plated vase with a cut-glass dish can be fitted on it for displaying fruit or sweetmeats.

This centrepiece is 46.5 cm (18¼ inches) tall and weighs almost 13 kg (30 pounds). Its solid appearance is normal for centrepieces made in this period.

The base is engraved in three places with the crest of the Earl of Portsmouth.

Shells and foliage, found in the spaces between the feet, are typical of the rococo style.

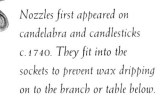

Nozzles first appeared on candelabra and candlesticks c.1740. They fit into the sockets to prevent wax dripping on to the branch or table below.

The six candle arms are of leaf-capped scrolling form, and each one has a circular socket and nozzle.

The cast feet have a lion mask and acanthus scrolls. Cast decoration is created by using a mould to make the relevant piece, then soldering it to the object.

The stem and base have applied decoration of cornucopiae, vines and fruits.

The underside of the base is stamped Rundell Bridge et Rundell Aurifices Regis et Principis Walliae Regentis (Rundell, Bridge and Rundell Goldsmiths to the King and the Prince of Wales Regent). Storr worked for these goldsmiths before he established his own firm, Storr & Mortimer.

GEORGE IV THREE-LIGHT CANDELABRA CENTREPIECE

Made by John Bridge in 1824, this candelabra is in the naturalistic style. Many of the flower heads and leaves on the stem and branches are removable, as is the fluted central bowl, which has a cut-glass liner. The drip pans have similar removable glass bowls. A coat of arms, crest and inscription were added in 1833. An inscription underneath the base reads Rundell Bridge et Rundell Aurifices Regis Londini, identifying the silversmith.

EMPIRE ORMOLU SURTOUT DE TABLE

A good example of the type of table centrepiece that was popular in early 19th-century Europe, this *surtout de table* has three sections and a gallery, with cast decorations of swag trophies alternating with anthemia. The glass and ormolu tazze, which would have held fruits or sweetmeats, are slightly later in date, but they give an idea of how these centrepieces were "furnished".

LOUIS PHILIPPE ORMOLU CENTREPIECE

This French piece, made c.1840, shows how styles became more eclectic. The scallop-shaped dish top is centred with bulrushes, with three wolfhounds peering into the dish; a feature that reflects the growing interest in naturalism as well as hunting. The bowl's hexagonal support ends in stylized dolphin masks. The inswept base, which has scrolled feet, echoes the mixture of decorative motifs.

SILVER SUBSTITUTES

As the 18th century progressed, the middle classes – who aspired to have the same things as those who were wealthier – sought a more affordable alternative to silver. Early in the 19th century, the development of silver lustre allowed potters such as Wedgwood to make ceramic copies of silver tea sets. These wares, of course, were not as durable as the substitutes made of metal.

Perhaps the most well-known silver substitute was Sheffield plate, used from the 1760s to produce both useful and ornamental wares. To create it, a silver sheet was applied to a copper ingot and the two were heated so that they fused together. The resulting combination of silver on copper was then rolled out into a sheet, ready to be shaped. This worked well except that the copper interior of open items, such as mugs and jugs, could be seen. To overcome this, the makers took two sheets of silver and sandwiched the copper between them. If the copper layer showed through, the copper was covered with silver wire, which was soldered into place.

Another metal substitute, called Britannia metal, first appeared in Sheffield *c.*1770. This was a pewterlike alloy of copper, tin and antimony (an alloy which resembles pewter). Another type of metal used was ormolu, which comes from the French words *or moulu* (ground gold). It is a term widely used to describe mounts for furniture and objects. The gilding, which can be applied to various metals, including bronze and brass, was applied using the noxious mercury or fire gilding process.

The mid-1840s saw the emergence of the process of electroplating, in which a coat of silver was applied by electrolysis to a base metal – such as copper or nickel. The new process eventually replaced the methods used before, including that of gilding metal.

GEORGE III CANDELABRA

All is not what it seems in this Sheffield plate five-branch candelabra, made c.1810. It is, in fact, a composite piece made from a pair of candelabras, whose components can be used in various combinations.

The central socket can be taken away to make a four-light centrepiece. The remaining components can be used in the form of a candlestick.

The overall appearance of the candelabra, including the foliage details on the branches, is in the Regency style.

The upper section, with two scrolling candelabra branches, can be removed and fitted on to the other candlestick to create two two-light candelabras or, with the central sockets, two three-light candelabras.

The stem and base is one of a pair of candlesticks.

One section with two candelabra branches is fitted into the top of the stem. Another branched section is fitted into the first one and topped with the central socket to form a five-light candelabra.

Sections of the base, stem, shoulders, sockets and nozzles are decorated with gadrooning.

SHEFFIELD PLATE CANDLESTICKS

These candlesticks, made in 1810, are telescopic. As the candle burns down, the stem of the candlestick can be pulled upward to maintain the height of the wick at a comfortable level. The minimum height of the candlestick is 20 cm (8 inches), and it can be extended to 28 cm (11 inches).

The top of the sockets are fitted with removable nozzles to prevent candle wax running down the stem.

As should be expected with antique Sheffield plate, the silver has worn away revealing the copper beneath. This is known as bleeding. Small amounts, as seen here, are acceptable.

The candlesticks have gadrooning around the base, stem, shoulder and sconce.

OLD SHEFFIELD PLATE ENTRÉE DISH

Entrée dishes were first introduced during the mid-18th century. This example dates from *c.*1840. Some had a warming stand, which could be filled with hot water in order to keep the food warm. The handle on this dish can be unscrewed so that the lid can also be used to serve food. It is also a practical idea for storing the dishes, since they normally came in pairs or larger numbers.

PAIR OF VASE-SHAPED WINE COOLERS

These partly reeded pieces, made of Sheffield plate *c.*1800, are a good example of the restrained decoration that was also found on silver at this time. The reeded handles with grapes and foliage emphasize their use. The collars and liners are removable – the collars concealed from view the ice packed around the liner.

FRENCH ORMOLU BOWL

One of a pair, this bowl, made *c.*1830, was used on the dining table for holding sweetmeats or fruit. Although the winged sphinx handles hark back to the Empire style, the osier-shaped body and moulded oval base and scroll feet are in the rococo revival style, which was becoming popular at this time. The bowl still has its original glass liner.

WINE WARES

Alcoholic beverages continued to play a substantial role in eating habits during the first half of the 19th century, and as the century progressed, the custom of serving a different wine with each course became established. As in the previous century, wine wares were manufactured in silver, ceramic and silver substitutes.

The range of items produced was quite extensive. Wine coolers, for example, were made in the more classical campana shape, which resembles an inverted bell. But some English silver wine coolers were copied from ancient classical vases, such as the Warwick vase – a marble vase from Hadrian's villa – and the Roman glass vase known as the Portland Vase.

In order to protect table tops from drips and spillage as decanters were passed around the table, wine coasters had been introduced in the second half of the 18th century, and their use became even more widespread. The use of decanters meant that there had to be some way of identifying the contents. To fill this need, silver or enamelled labels, with the name of the appropriate wine or liqueur, were suspended around the necks of the decanters by chains.

Brandy saucepans with small spirit lamps were, as in the past, used to warm brandy at the table. Although glasses had been used for the drinking of wine since the mid-18th century, silver goblets continued to be produced and used.

Beer jugs were still being made in pottery for the poorer households and in silver for the gentry. For wine, in addition to decanters, claret jugs in the shape of neoclassical ewers were made, often with very elaborate decoration, including scrolls, medallions and other classically inspired motifs. Some claret jugs were made of silver-mounted glass and copied the form of the ancient Greek *ascos*, a jug used for lamp oil.

GEORGE IV SILVER-GILT DOUBLE DECANTER TROLLEY

Benjamin Smith was responsible for producing this elaborate decanter trolley, one of a pair, in 1827. The decanters were placed in the coasters and the trolley could be rolled across the table.

Pierced silver-gilt vine tendrils in a naturalistic style form the sides of the coasters. To pierce the material, the silversmith would have used a chisel and hammer or a saw.

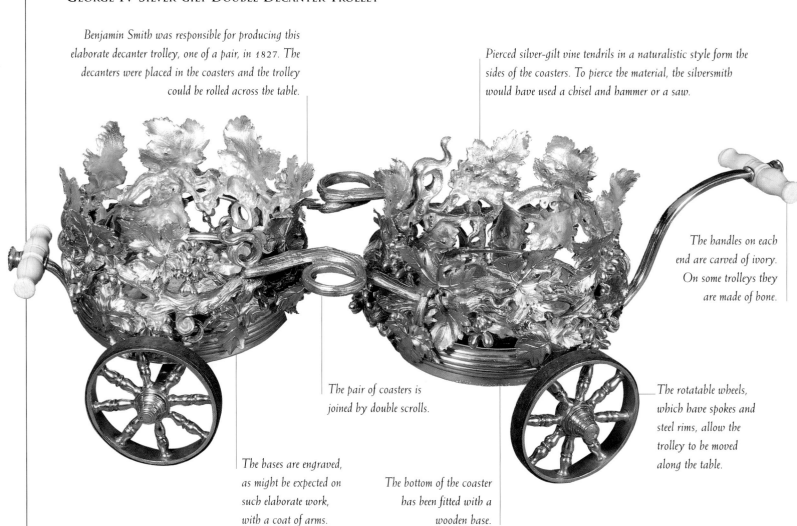

The handles on each end are carved of ivory. On some trolleys they are made of bone.

The pair of coasters is joined by double scrolls.

The rotatable wheels, which have spokes and steel rims, allow the trolley to be moved along the table.

The bases are engraved, as might be expected on such elaborate work, with a coat of arms.

The bottom of the coaster has been fitted with a wooden base.

GEORGE III WINE FUNNEL

Funnels were used to make decanting wine from its bottle easier. This funnel was made by Paul Storr in 1818.

The everted rim has shell, foliage and gadrooned decoration.

The partly fluted spigot is curved.

The strainer, designed to catch sediment and any pieces of cork when wine was being decanted from its bottle, is detachable so that it can be thoroughly cleaned after use.

GEORGE III SILVER-GILT WINE LABELS

These shaped labels, made by Paul Storr in 1818, have cast and chased decoration of shells, fruit, foliage and scrolls — suitable subjects for the table.

The chains attached to the labels allow them to be placed around the neck of a decanter.

Each label is stamped with the name of the wine, "Claret" and "Madeira", thus identifying the contents of the decanter.

GEORGE IV SILVER-GILT PUNCH SET

Punch, usually with a rum or brandy base, was a drink much enjoyed in polite society. This set of seven cups, the one in the centre being slightly raised on a pedestal, is decorated with trailing vines and a vine handle. The inner liner is removable to making cleaning easier. Berried laurel branches can be seen between the stands for the cups. It was made by Philip Rundell, of the goldsmiths Rundell, Bridge and Rundell, in 1820.

GEORGE III BEER JUG

This large pear-shaped jug stands on a circular spreading foot and has chased decoration of scalework panels, flowers and scrolls. The scrolls are echoed in the shape of the handle and the curved spout. The coat of arms was added in the 1830s. Although beer was drunk by both the rich and poor, such silver jugs would have been used in a wealthy household.

VASE-SHAPED WINE FOUNTAIN

By the early 19th century, such pieces were an anachronism and were no longer made, despite the Regency taste for large display silver. This fine example, which was ordered by Queen Anne as a gift, was made by Pierre Platel in 1713. The piece was modified in 1833: the tap through which the wine was poured was removed and a circular stand, made in the same style, was added so that the fountain could be used for display purposes.

OTHER USEFUL TERMS

ELECTROPLATING A process in which a coat of silver is applied by electrolysis to a base metal such as copper or nickel. An electroplated item has the appearance of being silver, without the expense of one made of solid silver.

MOKUME A Japanese decorative technique by which metal is worked to resemble wood.

PARIAN A fine, white semi-matt biscuit porcelain that was developed separately by Minton and Copeland. Parian was used largely for manufacturing busts and other sculptures, but it was sometimes used for making table ornaments.

DINNER SERVICE

The table is set with a Spode creamware dinner service. The large tureen would have been used for vegetables and the smaller tureen with the stand and the ladle would have been used for sauces.

SERVANTS

During this period there was a gradual change from having the serving dishes on the table – so that the diners helped themselves to the food – to being served by the servants in a style known as "dinner à la russe".

CARVING SET

On the rectangular platter are a steel carving knife and fork, with silver-mounted bone handles. These sets were part of the paraphernalia found on the Victorian table.

GLASSES

The traditional position for glasses was the right of the place setting. The number of glasses used reflects the fact that a different wine was served with each course.

CANDLESTICKS

The table was still set with candlesticks, although their role became somewhat more decorative because of the introduction of gas and, later, electricity.

THE REVIVALIST STYLES: 1840–1900

The 19th century was a period of social change. Great Britain led the way in the Industrial Revolution, which had begun the previous century, and there was a growing use of mechanical processes there and in other Western countries. These developments were reflected in the manufacture of ceramics and silver, and they helped fulfil the growing middle classes' demand for table and other wares.

It was a period of eclecticism, with many established styles being reinterpreted in a manner that clearly denoted their 19th-century origins: the wares typically have far more ornament than the originals on which they were based. Despite being based on earlier styles, these pieces have an individuality that makes them sought after today. French rococo, classical, Gothic and Renaissance motifs were all part of the decorative repertoire used and were styles favoured by the nouveau riche in the decoration of their homes. There was a vogue for naturalism, too, and fishwares and savoury wares were often shaped to reflect this interest. This period also saw a growth in the production of ceramics that were designed especially for children. They were usually decorated with subjects or mottoes that were felt to be appropriate to the upbringing and education of a 19th-century child.

CUTLERY
Spoons and knives were placed on the right-hand side of the plate and forks on the left. The utensils to be used first were placed the farthest away from the plate, so the diners worked their way from the outside in.

SEASONINGS
There was always more than one salt cellar (far left) on the table, as well as usually more than one mustard pot (left) and cruet, to save having to pass items up and down the table.

GOTHIC REVIVAL

In England, the re-emergence of an interest in the Gothic style can be traced back to the 18th century, when Gothic motifs once again appeared in furniture and the architecture of houses such as Strawberry Hill. The fascination with what some regarded as a national style grew in the 19th century and was seen as an antidote to the fashionable French Empire style and to classicism in general.

By the 1830s, there was an interest in the Gothic in France, where a form known as the Troubador style existed. Both these styles affected interior decoration, as well as exterior architecture. In addition to furniture and decorative items, useful tablewares were also made in what was believed to be the Gothic style. However, since most Gothic-style decoration looked back to church architecture for inspiration rather than domestic examples, craftsmen were actually producing a pastiche of the medieval original.

Some designers sought to "re-create" the style authentically. Probably the most well-known English exponent was Augustus Welby Northmore Pugin (1812–52), the son of a French emigré, who championed the restrained use of ornament. The decoration on his wares is sparse when compared with the products of other firms.

Although there was some interest in Gothic revival in the United States, it was overshadowed by interest in other revival styles, for example classical and rococo revival.

EARTHENWARE BREAD PLATE

This bread plate is the simplest of three versions designed by Augustus Pugin for the Minton factory. Here three colours – red, blue and buff – have been used; another version has six colours and one was produced in majolica glazes. Pugin's association with the Minton factory came about through his meeting Herbert Minton, the son of the original founder, while seeking someone to make tiles for him.

The careful use of decoration on this earthenware plate is typical of Pugin's work. He is normally associated with designing tiles and earthenware items.

The plate was a popular souvenir at the Great Exhibiton of 1851. People bought them at the Minton stand to take home.

A registration mark was introduced in 1842 to help protect copyright. The diamond-shaped mark on the back of the plate shows that it was registered on 4 March 1848.

The encaustic process, which was first used in medieval times, was used to make the plate. The process involves inlaying the body with different coloured clays and is more typically used for tiles.

The central medallion is
surrounded by sheaves of wheat,
an indication of the plate's
intended use for serving bread.
The decoration is simple,
reflecting Pugin's search
for authenticity.

Roundels, typical Gothic
decorative motifs, are drawn
from architecture and
stained-glass windows.

"Waste Not Want Not" is an
exemplary Victorian motto. Such
sayings were sometimes incorporated
in the decoration of rooms.

TEAPOT, MILK JUG AND SUGAR BOWL

Designed for the mass market, this tea service was made of Britannia
metal c.1840. The arched "blind window" panels on the octagonally
shaped bodies reflect church architecture – the details were derived
from windows and choir stalls. Many useful wares in Britannia metal
were exported to the United States.

SILVER-GILT AND ROCK-CRYSTAL BEAKER

The design of this beaker, made in
Europe in the early 19th century,
copies that of ones made in Germany
and Burgundy in the late 15th century.
From the swan feet upward, the quality
of the decorative work, which is set with
rubies, emeralds and baroque pearls,
indicates that the piece was not intended for
practical purposes but as a display item – it
is symbolic of wealth and power.

ORMOLU CANDELABRA

This three-light candelabra, one of a mid-
Victorian pair, is of Gothic form. It is
decorated with *champlevé* enamel, a type of
enamelling used in the Middle Ages. The
nozzles have Gothic-style piercing and the
drip pans have trefoil decoration, a feature
associated with church architecture. The
base is decorated with the English lion
and crowned mythical beasts.

RENAISSANCE REVIVAL

In the mid-19th century, the decorative arts of the Renaissance period caught the public's imagination, and it was not at all unusual to find the rooms in the house of a wealthy man decorated in differing styles. This renewed interest in the Renaissance led to the production of many ceramics decorated in that style.

In Italy, there was a resurgence of maiolica wares which copied those of the 15th and 16th centuries; and in Spain, there was a revival of Hispano-Moresque pottery. The wares of the French potter Bernard Palissy were also copied on both sides of the English Channel, as were the works of the Florentine Della Robbia. Some were 19th-century objects decorated in these historic styles; others copied the shapes of earlier pieces such as ewers and cups and covers. Saint-Porchaire work was also copied, but the decoration was mainly painted instead of inlaid, which was a far more laborious and costly technique.

In 1848, the Frenchman Léon Arnoux began work at the English factory of Minton, where he introduced a variation of ceramic known as majolica. This style was completely different from the Italian maiolica, although the name is a derivative. The earthenware body usually had relief decoration and was covered with several bright coloured glazes, and a whole variety of shapes and forms reflecting the differing styles were produced. This new majolica was first shown at the Great Exhibition of 1851 and was soon copied by other firms, such as George Jones and Wedgwood.

MINTON MAJOLICA CENTREPIECE

Many of the elements on this centrepiece by Minton were drawn from the Renaissance period. The naturalistic decoration also allows it to be regarded as an example of naturalism, highlighting how many pieces of this period were hybrids of differing styles.

The tiered column rising from the base is decorated with a basket-weave pattern in relief.

A fox's head and paws mark the division between the sections. A continuous swag around the base runs behind the heads.

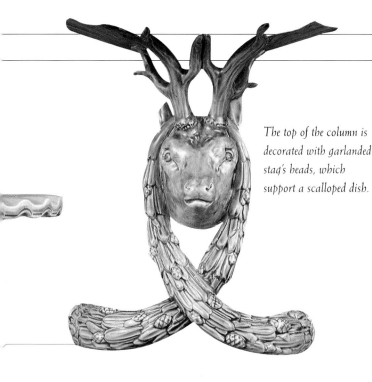

The top of the column is decorated with garlanded stag's heads, which support a scalloped dish.

MINTON TAZZA
Made in 1870, this tazza is an example of Henri Deux, or Saint-Porchaire, wares and is a copy of a 16th-century original. The decoration of scrolls and strapwork is painted rather than inlaid, as it would have been on an original piece. The tazza bears a paper label for the well-known London retailer T. Goode & Co, which still flourishes today.

The flower-shaped base is divided into six sections, which would probably have held fruit, flowers or sweetmeats.

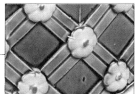

Latticework with daisies decorates the side of the base.

MINTON EWER
The decoration of this baluster-shaped ewer, with its trefoil neck and scrolling handle with a lion mask and ring, evokes the enamels produced at Limoges in France during the Renaissance period. The Minton artist Benjamin Lockett painted the white and gilt design of fleur-de-lys within a diaper pattern on a black background. The ewer was made c.1856.

Turquoise was one of the more popular colours used at the time.

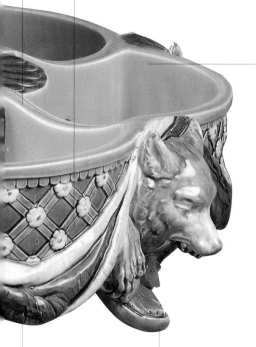

Six triangular feet decorated with moulded leaves support the base.

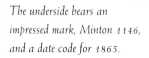

The underside bears an impressed mark, Minton 1146, and a date code for 1865.

DESSERT AND TABLE SERVICE CUTLERY
These forks and spoons have two different Renaissance-style patterns. The smaller dessert cutlery (left) bears the Bachanalian pattern; the larger table pieces are in the Staghunt pattern. Both sets date from the late Regency period and are composites – extra pieces have been added. It is always more desirable to have a set of one date rather than a composite one.

CLASSICAL REVIVAL

Favoured on both sides of the Atlantic, the classical revival style was really a continuation of the Empire style, but it grew heavier in form as the century progressed. Its advocates believed that the forms of classical art were the best and purest, and to the emerging newly prosperous classes it was, like the other revival styles, one that had a proven track record and was, therefore, "safe" to follow.

The increase in public museums during this period meant that visitors to them were able to see actual objects from the past, and they demanded a more authentic re-creation of the style through the use of decorative details. Classical motifs, such as palm leaves, paterae, husks and garlands, were used to decorate houses, rooms and the objects used within them, and classical statues were reproduced in both Parian, a type of fine white marble, and bronze.

The jasperwares of Wedgwood, which had first appeared during the 18th century, remained popular in the 19th, partly because their design was derived from the cameo glass of ancient Rome. Minton even produced a tableware pattern based on the design for the Sèvres service ordered by the Russian empress, Catherine the Great (see pp. 50–51).

Although the demands for authenticity of a more discerning public might suggest that reproductions were accurate copies of ancient wares, not everything in this period – with its many styles – was "pure". For instance, classical shapes could have Gothic or rococo decorative elements – Wedgwood even produced jasperware with naturalistic decoration.

NAPLES CREAMWARE PART TABLE SERVICE

These pieces were made in the late 19th century by the Giustiniani factory in Naples, which also copied Renaissance maiolica.

The depressed cylindrical form of the teapot possibly imitates the shape of an oil lamp.

The service includes small campana vases which would have been used on the table for flowers. Such vases are also found in some 18th-century services.

The Etruscan-style figurative decoration was copied from Greek vases. Although the decoration in general is inspired by classicism, it was inaccurately applied to the service – unlike the items on the right, which show the correct use of the antique.

The large bowls on stems would have been used for fruit.

Shallow two-handled stands were intended to hold sweetmeats.

All the plates have shaped rims and differing border designs. The borders, derived from ancient sources, incorporate paterae, lozenges, foliage, scrolls and flowers.

Some of the shapes used resemble those from ancient Greece. The deep two-handled bowls have decorated interiors.

WEDGWOOD CANDLESTICKS

These candlesticks, a pair from a set of four, are in the shape of Corinthian columns. They were made of black basalt, a hard stoneware, c.1885. The stems are accurately decorated with spiralling gilded garlands and the nozzles have sprigged decoration with gilt and bronzed leaves. Applied decoration on the square bases is of laurel swags suspended from bronzed ram's masks and gilt lozenges.

BERLIN ARMORIAL TUREEN, COVER AND PLINTH

The Berlin factory was well known for its services and this tureen comes from one made c.1820. It is an early example that illustrates the beauty of the classical style. The body is decorated with bronzed swags of fruit hung from satyrs' heads and supported by putti. Below is a band with blue scrolling foliage and roundels depicting the heads of cattle, sheep and deer on a *ciselé* gilt band. A similar band appears on the cover, which also has a band of bronzed flowers and foliage and a lion finial supporting a medallion with a chased coat of arms. The ribbed decoration on the plinth is broken by four rosettes.

PORTLAND VASE WINE COOLER

This cooler, which would have held a single bottle, is a rare silver-gilt example of this model in the classical revival style. It derives from the Roman blue-glass vase with white cameo decoration that was lent to the British Museum in 1810 by its owner, the Duke of Portland – hence the name. (A more common form was that of the Warwick Vase.) The original was made during the reign of Emperor Augustus (27 BC–AD 12); this vase was made by Philip Rundell in 1823.

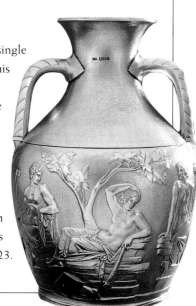

ROCOCO REVIVAL

The early 19th century saw the emergence in England of an interest in the arts of the *ancien régime*. This led to the revival of a style that was thought to be Louis XIV, but was actually more 18th century in feel, with its swirls and curves. French styles soon caught on and were copied in Europe and the United States for the rest of the century. The wealthy thought nothing of mixing authentic 18th-century pieces with modern 19th-century copies. Contemporary interior views, such as those of Empress Eugenie's apartments at St Cloud – which were decorated in the Louis XVI style, harking back to the 18th century – offer good examples of the tastes of the period.

The expansion of the middle classes and their desire to emulate those higher up the social ladder meant that there was a big demand to be satisfied. Factories such as Meissen in Germany reproduced many models from the 18th century, including figures and dinner services. However, the quality was no longer the same since new manufacturing processes were used that cut down on production time. Many other factories in Dresden and other parts of Germany also made cheaper imitations for the lower end of the market. The products of Sèvres were also much copied and imitated.

Metalwares were produced in this pervasive style too, but as so often happened in the 19th century, the decoration was usually overdone when compared with that found in the previous century. In some cases, pieces were made in a combination of styles; for example, a candelabra may have had a medieval figurative scene on its base, with candle branches in the rococo style.

A SET OF SILVER-GILT SALT CELLARS

These salt cellars were made in 1859 by C.F. Hancock. The group consists of two pairs, recalling the porcelain figures found on the 18th-century table. Such figural salt cellars were particularly popular in the 1850s and 1860s.

Hunting is the theme of the first pair. The lady falconer has a hooded falcon upon her arm.

The huntsman is modelled loading his gun.

The theme of the second pair is market sellers. The woman, who proffers a small bunch of flowers in her hand, is a flower seller.

The clothes are in the 18th-century style. Hancock incorporated many details into the dress, such as the buttons on the fruit seller's tight-fitting waistcoat and the lacing on the flower seller's bodice.

SWING-HANDLE CAKE BASKET

This silver basket, with pierced sides, was made in 1862. Although it is a good reproduction of a style that was popular in mid-18th century England, it has certain differences which indicate its later origin: the original baskets were wider and deeper.

DRESDEN SALT

This late 19th-century example is based on an original Meissen model. The salt would have been placed in the flower-adorned conch shell, which has a seated putto beside it. The shell and putto rest on a scroll-moulded base. Underneath are the blue initials AR, in a style similar to those of Augustus Rex found on some pre-1730 wares; they suggest that the salt may have been made at the Helena Wolfsohn factory in Dresden, where copies of 18th-century originals were made.

Each figure holds a basket with a rope-twist handle hanging from one arm. The interiors of the baskets are engraved with two crests and a coronet. The rope twist is also found around the top and base of each basket.

The fruit seller holds a bunch of grapes aloft.

SWEETMEAT FIGURES

This pair of figures of a man and woman are based on 18th-century models. They were manufactured at the Meissen factory c.1880 and sent to an outside workshop for decoration. The reclining figures are in floral costumes typical of the 18th-century style. The oval bowls, which would have held sweetmeats, are decorated with flowers and scattered insects. The figures and bowls are positioned on shaped bases, which have moulded scrolls highlighted in pink and gilt.

The salt cellars are covered in silver gilt to protect them from the corrosive effects of salt.

A chased circular base of simulated rockwork, scrolls and shells supports each figure.

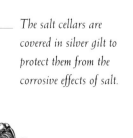

NATURALISM

The vogue for naturalism was particularly strong in the middle years of the Victorian era and can be found in most fields of the decorative arts. The designers used almost anything that could be interpreted in either plant or animal form, reflecting the prevailing interest in flora and fauna.

Of course, the style was not completely new. In the 18th century, potters and silversmiths had used plant and animal motifs to decorate their wares, for example, the crabstock spouts and handles found on English teapots and the *faux-bois* (false wood) borders found on services. This concept of painting or glazing borders to look like wood originated at the Niderviller factory in France but was copied elsewhere.

Wedgwood introduced the Nautilus shell into pottery designs in 1774 and many china examples were made in the 19th century. A type of flower-encrusted china, known as Coalport (in imitation of wares by Meissen and Dresden), was used to make baskets and some tea sets; they were not as practical as their silver counterparts. Majolica was a particularly good medium for depicting naturalism and various examples can be found, ranging from fish pickle dishes to plates with natural-looking pierced decoration in the form of holly.

In silverwares, shell shapes had long been used and their popularity continued in the 19th century. Services in the Vine pattern were popular, and the melon form – some with applied foliage and flowers – was common for teapots of this period. Conventionally shaped covered dishes were also made, with highly detailed silver handles in the shape of lobsters or some other crustacean.

The gourds are made of copper, and to create their woodlike appearance, a Japanese technique known as mokume was used (see p. 88).

SILVER AND MIXED-METAL COFFEE POT

This pot was designed by Edward C. Moore especially for the Paris Exhibition in 1878. Its Japanese-style decoration is an expression of the emerging Aesthetic style, but its shape is also a strong example of naturalism. The coffee pot bears the maker's mark for Tiffany & Co., New York, and a French control mark because it was imported into France.

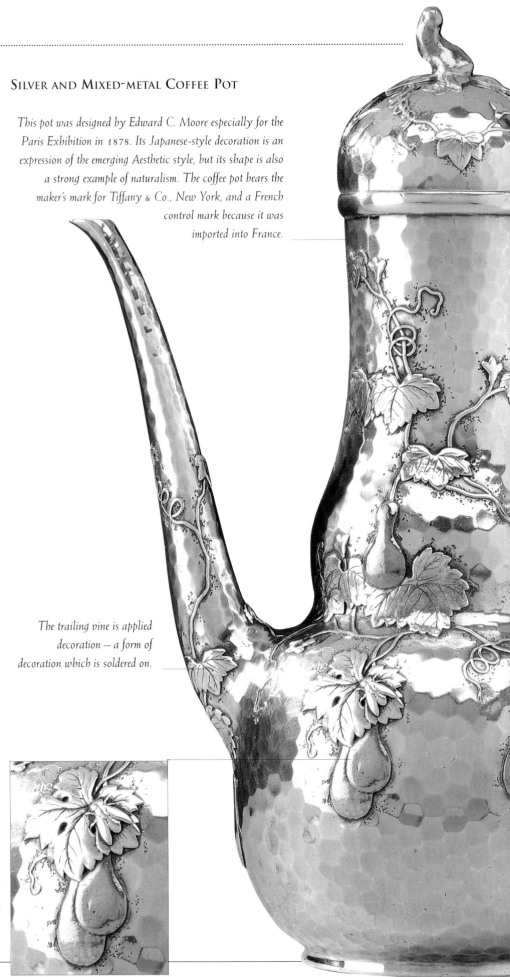

The trailing vine is applied decoration – a form of decoration which is soldered on.

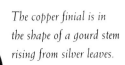

The copper finial is in the shape of a gourd stem rising from silver leaves.

The lid is decorated with entwined vines and a mokume butterfly is applied to the front.

The handle has two ivory rings, at the top and bottom, which are held in place by silver pegs, to insulate the handle from the heat of the beverage.

An applied beetle, which seems to be climbing upward, decorates the handle.

The decorative "dimpled" surface is created by spot-hammering.

The elongated gourd shape of the coffee pot is echoed in the applied decoration.

SHELL-SHAPED JUG

This Nautilus shell jug, with its coral-shaped handle, was made by the Belleek factory in Ireland and is easily recognized by its pearly lustrous glaze. Although it was made *c.*1910, this example is typical of the shell-shaped wares the factory had been producing since the 1860s. Similar wares were produced in the United States in the late 19th century.

SILVER BOWL ON FLUTED BALL FEET

Made *c.*1890, this bowl bears the maker's mark of the Whiting Mfg. Co. The circular body is decorated with repoussé and chased oyster, mussel and clam shells among seaweed. The wavy rim also adds to the marine effect. The use of repoussé chasing, in which hammering the metal produces a raised design that is then "pushed back in places", enables the silversmith to produce highly detailed work.

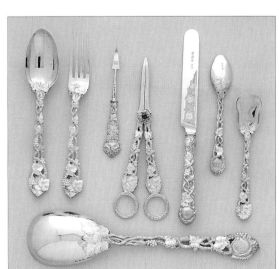

PARCEL-GILT SILVER DESSERT SERVICE

The service has openwork stems in the Vine pattern. It was made by Elkington & Co. and bears the London hallmark for 1890. Only part of this service for 18 is shown (from left): a dessert spoon and fork, a pick with a silver-gilt blade, grape scissors, a dessert knife with a parcel-gilt blade, a teaspoon, an ice-cream spoon and (bottom) a large serving spoon. The set includes a sugar sifter, sugar tongs and nutcrackers.

A FOCUS ON PLATES

Plates have been used in the home for hundreds of years. They come in at least six sizes, with the larger dinner plates being 23–25 cm (9–10 inches) in diameter; dessert and side plates are smaller. Some plates were made for display purposes. It wasn't until the 18th century that plates were made as part of a table service, which would have included serving dishes and other accessories, all with matching decoration.

Many of the early ceramic shapes were derived from contemporary silver plates – as well as from ones made of pewter and wood – and they were made with both plain and shaped rims. Decoration on silver plates was often limited to the rim. On ceramic plates, however, the decoration varies enormously – from the highly sophisticated examples which were made for the royal courts of Europe to the simple but elegant creamware ones made by Wedgwood and others. Armorials, flowers, birds, figures and landscape scenes are among the motifs used to adorn these items. Such decoration was often hand-painted in the 18th and 19th centuries, although many examples have transfer-printed decoration.

It is always more desirable to buy a complete set of plates, particularly if you plan to put them to practical use, but some single plates are worth purchasing for decorative purposes alone.

Ceramic plates

Early Italian display plate, with portrait of a man in the central panel, 1510

Portuguese display plate, with stylized lion in the central panel, early 17th century

Kraak Chinese export display plate, with peacock in a landscape, 1620

English tin-glazed earthenware, or maiolica, display plate, c.1660

Kakiemon plate, with a man in front of a mountain, 1720

Vienna Du Paquier lobed-rim plate, with flowers in the central panel, c.1730

German blue and white plate with Chinese decoration by Meissen, c.1735

English delft plate, with a castle in the central panel, c.1740

French porcelain plate, with flowers and geometrically decorated rim, c.1760–70

Worcester plate in the Japanese Imari style, 1765

French plate featuring a stylized bird in a landscape, 1770

Chinese export blue and white porcelain plate, with floral decoration, c.1770

Staffordshire leaf-moulded plate, c.1840–80

French Quimper plate, c.1875

Sèvres plate decorated in the Japanese taste, c.1880

British display plate by William de Morgan, 1888–98

Silver plates

English silver-gilt plate, with a leaf border on the rim, 1690

Silver-gilt plate from Augsburg, c.1730

French plate by Jacques Roettiers, 1735–38

Lobed plate by Jacques-Nicolas Roettiers (Jacques' son), 1770

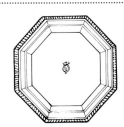

English octagonal plate by Tomas Heming, 1780

Kangxi famille verte plate, with a central panel of a bird on a branch, 1662–1722

English earthenware display plate from Staffordshire, featuring a mermaid, c.1675

Dutch Delft display plate from the Koeks factory, with panels of Romans, 1690

French faience plate, with a hunting scene, late 17th or early 18th century

Dutch Delft plate, with a basket of flowers, early 18th century

British delft polychrome display plate, featuring a man outdoors, c.1710

Meissen plate, with a shaped rim and decorated with flowers, 1745

English plate made at the Bow factory, with a couple on a bench, 1756

Chelsea plate, featuring birds and a border of flowers, c.1758

Salt-glazed plate from Staffordshire, with moulded decoration on the rim, 1760

Qianlong famille rose armorial plate, c.1760

Nymphenburg plate with flowers and insects, 1760–65

Wedgwood Queensware plate, featuring animals and a man in a landscape, 1775

English pearlware plate, with decoration in the Chinese style, c.1780–90

Scandinavian faience plate, with a leaf border, late 18th or early 19th century

Swansea plate, with simple flower decoration, 1800–10

Ridgway plate, with Beauties of America pattern, c.1820

English plate from the Coalport factory, 1820–25

Vienna-style cabinet plate, with a portrait of woman, 1890

Russian plate, with the hammer, sickle and star, c.1920

Queen Anne shaped plate, with floral bouquets, 1926

Art Deco Queen Anne shaped plate, 1932

Ridgway Homemaker plate in collage style, c.1950

French plate with a beaded edge, 1788

English Regency style plate, 1815

English plate inlaid with gold insects, 1878

American silver-gilt plate made for J.P. Morgan, c.1895

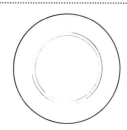

Scandinavian plate by Johan Rohde and Georg Jensen, c.1945

FISHWARES

In Catholic countries, fish has long been an important part of the weekly diet because it was customary not to eat meat on Fridays. In the early 19th century and before, our ancestors ate either freshwater fish or fish from the sea, depending on where they lived; those who did not live near a water source ate fish only rarely.

In the second half of the 19th century, however, changes in fishing occurred, with steam trawlers replacing sailboats and ice being used to preserve fish, both on the boat and during transportation from fishing ports to inland areas. This meant that sea fish became more widely available to all strata of society and it was no longer as expensive. Ice was even exported from Scandinavia to warmer countries where it was more of a rarity. The spread of the railway network saw previously small ports, such as Lowestoft on the Suffolk coast, grow into large fishing centres with trawler fleets.

One development as a result of the growth in fish eating was the introduction of fish knives and forks as part of flatware services. The fish slice – now with an accompanying fork – used for serving fish was usually a composite part of the service as well. The fish was generally served in a dish, either silver or ceramic, which had a strainer so that excess fish juices would drain into the dish below.

The idea of dining out grew during the 19th century and fish was sometimes served as an appetiser while waiting for dinner. The custom of eating savouries, which often featured such fish as sardines and anchovies, at the end of a meal also gained popularity.

MINTON MAJOLICA OYSTER STAND

The Minton factory produced this oyster stand in 1862, which is based on ceramic oyster stands made in France during the 18th century. There was a vast production of oyster wares during the 1850s and 1860s.

There are four tapering tiers of oyster shells.

The individual shells rest on nests of seaweed.

Although oysters had been eaten by all levels of society in the 18th century, they had become scarcer in Great Britain by the end of the 19th century due to the same type of problems faced today – pollution and over-harvesting. As a result, at the end of this period only the more wealthy could afford to eat them served on an oyster stand such as this.

The handle consists of three fish and an eel.

Each shell would have held an oyster, probably still in its own shell. There is room for about two-and-a-half dozen oysters.

The shells are realistically decorated: the rough exteriors are painted brown, the smooth interiors white.

The stand rests on a metal-mounted foot, which was constructed so that the stand could be revolved.

MINTON MAJOLICA SEAFOOD DISH

This piece, made at the Minton factory in 1859, shows the naturalistic elements often found in such wares. The cover of the central portion, in the shape of a large crab resting on seaweed, conceals a turquoise glazed interior. Fronds of seaweed are draped over the crab's back to form the cover's handle. The outer band of dark blue and brown containers is divided by rope twists; a single rope continues around the dish's edge to form a scalloped rim. The dish would probably have been used to serve shellfish such as mussels.

SARDINE DISH AND COVER

The cover of this electroplated sardine dish is decorated with a sardine fish and shells. The piece was made by Walker and Hall of Sheffield *c.* 1900. The dish, which would have contained a glass liner, has a ledge to hold the serving tongs, which have fish-shaped ends that match the one on the cover.

FISH SLICE FROM THE NEWTON TABLE SERVICE

This fish slice, one of four, is in the traditional form and has a shaped edge that was designed to ease the fish from the bone instead of cutting it. It is from a service made by John and Henry Lias in 1821 for the wedding of William John and Mary Ann Legh. Their son became the baron of Newton-in-Makerfield and each piece in the service bears the crest or arms of Newton. The design is in the King's pattern, and the pieces have also been cast with foliage.

CHEESEWARES

For many years, until the development of factory processes in the 1870s, cheese had been enjoyed mostly by landowners with great houses and by farmers because they were the ones with the dairies necessary for its production. The dairy was looked upon as the province of the lady of the house, and some women of high standing – Marie Antoinette is perhaps the best-known example – had their own specially built dairy so that they could escape into "rustic life".

Both hard and soft cheeses were made, and during the first half of the 17th century the consumption of cheese was still confined to locally made cheeses. The establishment of cheese fairs, such as the one held in the Oxfordshire town of Burford, meant that different varieties became better known over a slightly wider area. The market for cheeses continued to grow, and the restoration of the British monarchy in 1660 brought with it an introduction of European cheeses to Great Britain. It was during this period that cheese recipes first became available.

By the end of the 18th century, it was customary to serve cheese after dinner, and as a reflection of this, cutlery services now included cheese knives. On the 19th-century table, whole cheeses were usually served at meals in large cheese bells, but smaller covered cheese dishes, sometimes of segment shape to hold smaller pieces of cheese, were also made and used. Cheeses, including Stilton, Cheddar, Cheshire and Gloucester, were now regularly transported to London and other large towns to meet the ever-increasing orders.

CHEESE BELL AND STAND

This cheese bell and stand, made in the late 19th century, is in blue jasper and copies the Wedgwood jasperwares of the late 18th century. Copies of jasperware are usually not of the same high quality as the Wedgwood originals.

The dish was designed to hold a whole Stilton or hard cheese.

Bands of anthemion and bell flowers radiate from the central knop of the cover – these are typical examples of neoclassical ornamentation.

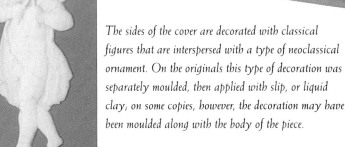

The sides of the cover are decorated with classical figures that are interspersed with a type of neoclassical ornament. On the originals this type of decoration was separately moulded, then applied with slip, or liquid clay; on some copies, however, the decoration may have been moulded along with the body of the piece.

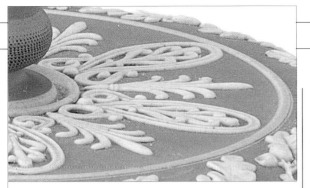

Jasperware is a type of stoneware invented by Wedgwood. At first, it was stained with metal oxides to give it its colour, but after 1777, the body may have been dipped in a coloured slip. White relief decoration was then applied. The blue seen here is the most common colour, and the finish is typically matt, although it is sometimes burnished for a glossy finish.

MAJOLICA CHEESE BELL
Made by the George Jones factory during the 1870s, this cheese bell is an example of the Gothic style. It is modelled as a stone tower, complete with ivy and ferns, and has a crenellated top and "arrow slits" in the sides, which would have served as ventilation holes to allow the cheese to breathe. The handle is in the form of a kneeling figure.

TOASTED CHEESE DISH
This oval Sheffield plate dish for toasting cheese was made c.1820. These cheese dishes were used to serve the cheese and usually have a wooden handle to allow the dish to be carried to the table without burning the carrier's hands. There is a concealed reservoir in the lower portion which was filled with hot water to keep the cheese warm. Such dishes were also made in a rectangular form.

SILVER CHEESE SCOOPS
Scoops were used both to taste the cheese to test its ripeness and as a server. Because cheese was consumed in small amounts at the end of a meal, these utensils were ideal. Both of the scoops date from c.1880: the bottom one has a turned ivory handle, the top one, a fiddle-shaped handle. Some large cutlery services included scoops, which are about 25 cm (10 inches) in length.

The base and lid have borders decorated in a leaf pattern.

SWEETS ACCESSORIES

Desserts and other sweetmeats continued to be appreciated into the 19th century and the choice was often quite extensive. For dessert, dinner guests were offered a bewildering array of cakes, biscuits, sweet and savoury jellies, iced puddings, trifles, blancmanges and compotes of fruit – all served on silver or ceramic dishes and stands in the differing forms and styles of the day. Fresh or preserved fruits were also served, and sometimes sorbets were consumed between the main courses to cleanse the palate.

Eating habits had gradually changed and dinner was now being served at a later hour (and lasting longer), yet lunch was not a substantial meal. As a result, people felt the need for some type of nourishment during the course of the afternoon, and so it became customary for tea to be served in the late afternoon. In some houses it was served in the drawing room, but in others it was a grander affair, laid out in the dining room. Sandwiches, biscuits and cakes were among the fare offered to help keep hunger pangs at bay.

Although the taking of afternoon tea started in the houses of the great, it was soon adopted by the middle classes. The idea of having a matching silver tea service, which had been extant since the end of the 18th century, grew in popularity in the 19th century. Such sets typically consisted of a matching teapot, milk jug and sugar bowl, as well as a hot water jug, which was sometimes used as a coffee pot. In wealthier houses, there was also a matching tray and even a tea urn.

SWEETMEAT DISH

The design of this sweetmeat dish is typically Victorian: it combines elements of Gothic, Renaissance and other styles. Such a dish would have held candied fruits, dried fruits, nuts or some other form of dry sweetmeat.

The silver-gilt stem is in the form of a kneeling winged putto, whose upstretched arms support the bowl. There are many 18th- and 19th-century sweetmeat dishes with figural supports, usually in the rococo style.

Because the crevices between the panels are so difficult to reach, the silver gilt in them is difficult to clean and has become tarnished.

The hallmark can be seen on the front of the base. It bears the maker's mark of Charles Rawling & William Summer and indicates that the piece was made in London in 1839.

The crenellated rim around the bowl is inset with semiprecious stones, including lapis lazuli and malachite.

The oval bowl balancing on the head of the putto is made of agate, which appears almost translucent.

The underside of the bowl's circular support is decorated with foliage that matches the pattern on the base.

The sweetmeat dish stands 12 cm (4¼ inches) high. Normally dishes such as these would have been made in pairs or sets and formed part of the table decoration.

Panels of semiprecious stones, or hardstones, are set into the hexagonal silver-gilt base.

The base is surrounded with engraved decoration of foliage. A scriber, a type of sharp tool, would have been used to remove the metal by hand.

SUGAR CASTER AND BOWL

The caster (right) was made in the 19th century, but is in the traditional baluster shape used since the 18th century. The pierced lid is a normal feature for such pieces, which would have been used at the dinner table for shaking sugar, over fruit for example. The bowl, with its tongs for picking up sugar lumps, is from a rococo revival tea set made by the Sheffield firm of Roberts and Slater in 1846. Such open bowls were typically used at the tea table.

MAJOLICA STRAWBERRY DISH

Made in 1868 by George Jones, this ceramic dish is in the shape of an oval yellow wicker basket with strawberries, blossoms and leaves moulded in relief. Attached are two smaller jars, with pink interiors, standing in wells that match the basket. Each jar has a spoon, formed as sprays of leaves tied with blue ribbons. The jars would have held cream and sugar – one spoon is pierced for the sugar – and the strawberries would have been placed in the dish.

BISCUIT BARREL

An example of German Art Nouveau, this silver biscuit barrel was made toward the end of the 19th century by the firm of J.P. Kayser. The flowing natural shape is typical of the products they produced in pewter under the name Kayserzinn. Biscuit barrels were made in a whole range of materials, including silver, glass, pottery and china.

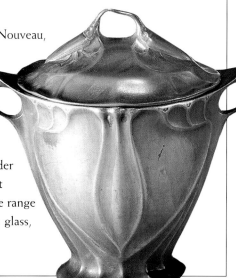

SAVOURY ACCESSORIES

By the 19th century breakfast in England had become a more substantial meal. Alongside the, by now, traditional toast with jam or marmalade, a whole variety of other dishes were offered, such as eggs, sausages, bacon, chops and kidneys. All these were served in dishes that often had a lamp or warmer below. Special service sets were made in both metal and ceramic, and they were also used for supper. Some silver or plated supper sets also have cruets.

During this period, the Napoleonic wars led to the introduction of a tax on flour in Great Britain: this meant that large pastry-crust pies could no longer be made. To compensate, the Staffordshire potters made ceramic versions of the crusts and decorated them on the outside with appropriate motifs. Some were made in ironstone, which was strong enough to withstand the oven's heat, others were purely decorative.

Roast chestnuts were a delicacy that had been enjoyed since the 18th century, when special pierced ceramic baskets were made to hold them. This tradition carried on into the 19th century, with such firms as Minton producing majolica examples with chestnuts and their leaves, modelled in relief, forming part of the decoration. In addition, there were numerous shaped dishes, bowls and plates for pickles and sauces, all of which were a necessary adjunct to the meal.

It was also at this time that the idea of having a special carving knife and fork grew, and many decorative sets were made.

MINTON GAME PIE DISH AND COVER

The dish and cover is an amusingly decorated piece from the Minton factory and was made in 1877. "Coming through" the top of the cover, which has scattered flowers, are two hare's heads and a pair of duck's heads. They are realistically modelled and indicate that the dish was meant for game pie.

The hares' ears, which meet in the centre, would have been used as a handle to raise the cover.

The cover has a piecrust edge. A piece such as this would not have been ovenproof. The "pie" would have been made in a separate liner dish and, when cooked, would have been brought to the table concealed under this decorative cover.

MINTON PIGEON PIE TUREEN AND COVER

This model was designed c.1851 and, as its decoration suggests, was used to serve pigeon.

The domed cover is surmounted by a resting pigeon on a "bed" of green leaves.

The circular tureen and cover are moulded to resemble a wicker basket.

Around the base of the basket are four pigeons perched on logs, which are part of a nest of gnarled branches and leaves.

The side of the shaped moulded cover is decorated with a pair of green leaves, with pinkish brown beaded panels between them.

The dish has a platelike base that resembles basket weave with rope twist handles.

SILVER-GILT BREAKFAST SERVICE

Made by the Parisian firm of Puiforcat in the late 19th century, this breakfast service is similar to one made for Napoleon I. The central bowl and cover are surrounded by covered dishes and all are on a revolving stand. The dog-shaped handles on the dish covers are removable, as is the bud finial on the bowl's cover. The covers are engraved with anthemia and stylized foliage borders. Some services were made in ceramic fitted in a wooden or metal tray.

ARGYLE GRAVY JUG

This early 19th-century blue and white transfer printed jug is believed to be named after an 18th-century Duke of Argyll. Hot water would have been placed in the central compartment to keep the gravy in the outside compartment warm.

SILVER-PLATED EGG CODDLER

Inside the domed cover is a rack to hold four to six eggs to be cooked for breakfast. The eggs were boiled when the spirit lamp below the coddler was lit. The finial on the cover is in the shape of a bird standing over a nest, protecting its eggs. The base of the stand and the cover are decorated with bands of gadrooning. Some rare examples are fitted with an egg timer.

OUTDOOR EATING

The habit of occasionally eating outside the house is a long-established one among the upper classes in England. During the 16th century it was not unusual for the dessert course to be served in a pavilion, often specially constructed for the purpose, in a part of the garden or park surrounding a great house. In some late-Victorian photographs, formally dressed people can be seen sitting around a table that has been brought out from the drawing room into the garden to allow the family to take afternoon tea outdoors. The tea was served in exactly the same way as if it were taken indoors, with a silver tea service and fine china cups, saucers and plates.

Conservatories and winter gardens were popular places for such repasts too and even for dances. Indeed, a watercolour painted in 1854 by Charles Giraud shows the dining room of the Princess Mathilde in Paris, where a sumptuously laid table stands in the middle of what is obviously a winter garden, with banks of flowers and plants all around and a glass roof above.

Eating while fox-hunting has also long been a tradition, with not only the hunt breakfast beforehand but also the stirrup cup being passed around before the hunt set out. During the shooting parties of late Victorian and Edwardian England, lunch was taken either in an estate cottage or in the open air, with the food being served from silver or silver-plated dishes on to porcelain plates with all the panache that was found in the dining room back at the big house.

In the 18th century, a fitted travelling case or box was a necessity for both soldiers on campaign and for travellers. As the 19th century progressed, comfortable hotels – which took the place of the earlier coaching inns – were established, and travelling sets became less essential for the monied traveller.

TRAVELLING SERVICE

This set may well have been made for an officer to take on active service or on manoeuvres. It consists of a silver teapot, milk jug, sugar bowl, salt cellar, egg cup and cutlery.

Any porcelain – cup, saucer and plates – would have been kept in a separate case.

The handles of the teapot and milk jug and the knop on the teapot's lid are made of ivory.

Gilding on the interior of the salt cellar prevents corrosion; it has its own spoon.

It is always more desirable to have a travelling set in its case, even though, as here, the case is badly worn.

This set was made c.1890 and retailed by the Viennese firm of J. C. Klinkosch, whose full name can be seen stamped on the lining of the lid.

The interior of the case is moulded to create a snug fit for each of the various components of the set. The case has a pair of latches to hold the lid in place, as well as a lock in the centre.

The interior of the egg cup is gilded to prevent tarnishing from certain food chemicals.

The sugar bowl has a plain, unadorned form and two handles.

The set contains a knife, fork, egg spoon and teaspoon.

STIRRUP CUP

This finely modelled and chased silver stirrup cup in the form of a stag's head, with antlers of 14 points, was made by the leading silversmith, John S. Hunt. It bears a London hallmark for 1864 and is stamped with the name Hunt and Roskell. Ceramic versions were also made. The contents of the stirrup cup varied in different parts of Great Britain but could include combinations of port and brandy, gin and ginger wine or vodka and sherry. One concoction in Northumbria, known as a Percy Special, featured whisky and cherry brandy.

LATE VICTORIAN SILVER FLASKS

Sportsmen today still use flasks of this type, the contents providing a welcome warmer on a wet, cold day. Such flasks were either made entirely from silver or had an inner glass container. They were usually slightly curved to fit more comfortably against the body. The base could often be pulled off, as shown here, to provide a drinking cup. Both flasks were made in the late 19th century; the initialled one is less collectable than the earlier plain one.

WICKER PICNIC BASKET

Although not complete, this picnic basket gives an idea of the type used for outdoor meals earlier this century. The interior is fitted with flasks, sandwich boxes and other containers for food. The space between the two sets of flatware on the lid would have held the plates, and there is also a corkscrew. The basket bears the stamp "A. Barrett & Sons, Manufacturers, 63–64 Piccadilly".

SILVER FLASK

Made in Glasgow in 1872, this tapering flask would have been carried in a special holster by a huntsman or a member of a shooting party. The screw-top lid is attached to the body by a ring and chain to prevent it from being lost. The contents – probably whisky in this instance – would be poured into the removable tumbler that forms part of the base.

ARTS AND CRAFTS

Not everyone appreciated the ever-growing excesses of design during this period and, as a result, the English style known as the Arts and Crafts Movement emerged in the second half of the 19th century. Its exponents were men, such as William Morris and John Ruskin, who adopted Augustus Pugin's idea that craftsmanship and good, simple decoration were needed to show up the excesses of the mass-produced mainstream items being manufactured for the middle classes.

The Arts and Crafts message reached the United States, where Frank Lloyd Wright was perhaps the leading designer. However, the belief in using traditional methods of construction limited the market to the more wealthy, although some designs filtered down to the mass-produced market.

The re-emergence of Japan into the Western world at the 1862 International Exhibition, held in London, led to a new interest in Japanese decorative arts. The decoration on silver and ceramic tablewares became simpler and incorporated Japanese-style motifs. Gone were the formal patterns of rococo and Renaissance revivals and in their place were abstract patterns of such items as bamboo and birds. Sometimes silver and ceramics were decorated en suite.

Major manufacturers, such as Worcester, Minton and Copeland, began to produce such wares and even Wedgwood succumbed to producing Japanese-inspired pieces. Middle Eastern designs were popular in France, but wares in the Japanese style were also produced at various factories there, including Sèvres. Supporters of this Japanese style were adherents of what is known as the Aesthetic Movement and included Oscar Wilde and the painter Whistler. It also had its detractors – for example, Gilbert and Sullivan, who parodied its refined style in *Patience*.

LONGWY POTTERY CABARET

The set, which consists of a teapot, milk jug, sugar bowl and two cups, also has a tray. It was made at the Longwy factory in France c.1880.

The popularity of cabarets, in use since the 18th century, continued into the 19th. Also known as a tête à tête, the cabaret was a set for two people, and was usually used in less formal settings, such as a boudoir. Saucers were sometimes included in the set.

Islamic designs similar to this one were copied in other countries, such as England and the United States.

The set, instead of having a mass-produced look typical of factory wares, reflects the individuality of design and decoration found in the Arts and Crafts Movement.

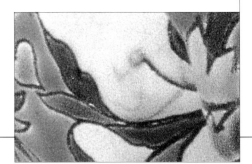

Although the pieces are not enamelled, the colourful decoration on this set resembles the enamel technique cloisonné, in which different enamel colours are separated by metal bands.

Tea Caddy

Produced by the Gorham Manufacturing Company of Providence, Rhode Island, *c.*1895, this tea caddy is an example of *japonisme*. It is made of silvered metal with a hammered finish and is inlaid in silver with branches, a bird and a butterfly. Gorham made silver in the many styles of the 19th century, and its pieces were considered to be second only to Tiffany's.

Electroplated Toast Rack

This toast rack was designed for the Birmingham firm of Hukin and Heath by Christopher Dresser. Like many leading Arts and Crafts designers, Dresser wanted to "reform" design, but – unlike them – he sought to bring these new simple and practical designs to the world of mass-production instead of confining them to the small specialist workshops and potteries.

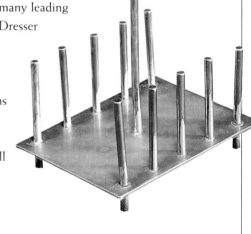

The use of strong glazes was popular in Arts and Crafts ceramics. Many European pieces were made with glazes based on the monochromes found in the ceramics of the Far East.

The Longwy factory was founded in the late 18th century, but it did not achieve recognition until it produced wares decorated in the Islamic manner, like these.

Plate and Sauce Boat

These pieces come from a set made by the Staffordshire-based Old Hall Earthenware Co. Ltd *c.*1880. They are an example of tableware with Japanese designs made for the mass market – this is the Hamden pattern. The set was designed by Christopher Dresser, whose visit to Japan in 1876–77 influenced some of his designs.

TIFFANY

In the classic film *Breakfast at Tiffany's*, the character Holly Golightly eats a pastry and drinks coffee while looking at a display of jewellery in a window of Tiffany's New York shop. If Holly could have afforded it, she could have gone in and bought a silver plate to eat off – since its opening in 1837, Tiffany has also sold tablewares.

Founded by Charles Lewis Tiffany, the company had by the middle of the 19th century become the leading American retailer and manufacturer of silver and jewellery. A number of leading designers of the era, such as Edward C. Moore, were among its staff. Its clientele was found both at home in the United States and in Europe – there were branches in Paris and London. The firm also showed at various international exhibitions, including the 1867 Paris Exhibition, at which they were awarded a prize for silverwares. The international high regard for Tiffany's wares is epitomized by the Royal Warrants it held, including one granted by Queen Victoria in 1883.

The pieces Tiffany produced ranged from those in the Aesthetic style to those in the more general historical revivals of the period. Patrons included John Pierpont Morgan, the Astors, the Vanderbilts and other luminaries of the Gilded Age. The mining magnate John Mackay had Tiffany make him a substantial table service featuring candelabras using silver from his Nevada mines, and it was not unknown for a customer to commission a service in gold.

Louis Comfort Tiffany, the son of the founder, is well known for his Art Nouveau glass and jewellery designs.

COPPER AND SILVER COFFEE SERVICE

This set bears the Tiffany & Co. maker's mark for c.1879. American manufacturers were able to use base metals, including copper, in their silver pieces because they were not bound by the strict hallmarking regulations that applied in Great Britain.

The silver handles of both the jug and coffee pot are marbled with gold and copper. The two ivory rings on the coffee pot's handle provide insulation from the heat.

Each piece has a silver rim and foot. The foot is inlaid with copper ornament in various geometric shapes. The inlaid metalwork technique was influenced by the Japanese, and the style was popular in Europe at the time.

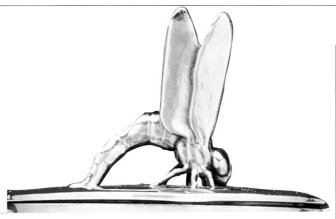

SILVER PICKLE DISHES

These elegant canoe-shaped dishes, each standing on four ball feet, were used on the dining table to hold various types of pickles. The surface of the silver has been spot-hammered and one dish has an applied frog while the other has a pickle. The dishes bear the Tiffany & Co. maker's mark for the period from 1878 to 1891.

Like the handle and spout, the lid of the coffee pot is decorated with gold and copper marbling. The main feature on the lid, however, is the exquisite silver dragonfly finial.

The spout is described in Tiffany's records as shaped like a "gutter spout", probably because of its long tapering form.

Each piece has a copper body, which is inlaid with silver and gold marbling, and applied decoration in the form of silver dragonflies.

COVERED SUGAR BOWL

This sugar bowl is part of an eight-piece silver tea and coffee service, made c.1852, which belonged to William Backhouse Astor and his wife, the legendary Mrs Astor. It is in the rococo revival style and has elaborate *repoussé* and chased foliate vine decoration. It bears the maker's mark of John C. Moore and three pieces are marked with the name Tiffany, Young and Ellis (the firm's original name); the other pieces are marked Tiffany & Co.

Like the coffee pot and sugar bowl, the cream jug has a tapering cylindrical form and is decorated in the Japanese taste so liked by the Aesthetic Movement. The dragonflies are just one example of the movement.

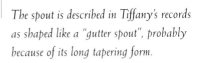

SILVER TUREEN, COVER AND STAND

Tiffany & Co.'s mark for 1862–70 appears on this neoclassical style tureen, which measures 37cm (15 inches) from handle to handle. Applied bands of flower heads in a geometric design appear below the rim and on the stand. Egg and dart bands also decorate the area below the rim and around the foot. The domed cover rises to a pedestal with a sheep as the finial. The tureen has a plated liner to keep the contents hot and to protect the interior of the tureen from corrosion.

CHILDREN'S WARE

Today, children are an integral part of family life, and they often have the chance to spend time with one parent or the other during the day. Things were not always so, for in the second half of the 19th century a nursery system was the norm for the children of the more affluent.

In a large household, nurses – or nannies as they are now more commonly known – would probably have had a nursery maid and possibly an under-nurse to assist them. Between them they would have been responsible for the day-to-day upbringing of the children in their care. Children saw their parents only rarely, either when the parents visited the nursery or if the children were allowed downstairs for a fleeting visit to the grown-up world.

Education was an important aspect of nursery life and it was one that spread to mealtimes – the children ate within the confines of their small world. The Staffordshire potteries and others manufactured a series of wares especially for the nursery, usually with transfer-printed decorations. Some of these wares depicted religious texts and mottoes, while others were adorned with scenes from children's books so that, even when eating, the Victorian child had the opportunity to improve his or her mind. The world of nature was also a popular theme, as the decoration on many pieces shows.

The popularity of children's ware has not waned, for, as is evident from the novelty wares of the 1920s and 1930s, firms continued to produce suitable items for children, but perhaps with a greater sense of fun than shown in some of the earlier Victorian examples. Today, as well as the more informal products associated with the latest cinema hit aimed at children, such enduring designs as the characters created by Beatrix Potter are still made, as is Royal Doulton's Bunnykins ware.

CHILDREN'S PLATES

These plates are examples of the type of wares that would have been found in a children's nursery in Great Britain and continental Europe during the mid to late 19th century.

The rim of the plate has a wavy edge and a moulded border decorated with leaves and cornucopia.

The central scene shows a group of children in a garden. The motto, in German, is "Youthful pleasure; what a boy does not learn a man does not know".

The central scene shows a blacksmith's workshop with some beehives behind it – both of which emphasize the point of the motto.

Made for the German market, this plate bears one of the popular mottoes that were meant to inspire a sense of duty in the user – it translates as "Diligence pays dividends but idleness causes debts".

This plate has the potter's name, John Wilkinson, and the date August 10, 1836 incised on the back. It also bears the impressed mark Wedgewood, which was used by the Stockton pottery of William Smith & Co. for a brief period – until the Wedgwood firm took action to prevent them from using it.

INFANCY

In the centre, a partly coloured image depicts a group of
children with one of them holding a bird's nest, in which
are two baby birds. The scene is appropriately entitled
Infancy and shows the sentimentality that was common at
the time. Surrounding the central panel is a floral border,
the top of which is broken by a bird – presumably the
mother of the two fledglings.

The rim of this plate is decorated with a
moulded border of colourful stylized flower
sprays in green, pink and blue.

INFANCY

A moulded garland and
medallion border decorates the
rim on this plate.

CHILD'S SMALL PLATE

A floral garland with coloured florets decorates the moulded border
of this plate. The central scene, entitled Sit Up Pompey, depicts
children with a begging dog. The plate, which was made by Powell
& Bishop in the 19th century, was also made in a larger version.

PORCELAIN MUG

Some children's ware depict historical personages. The scene in
purple lustre and manganese print on this somewhat sophisticated
china mug – which has a spur-eared handle – depicts a boy, wearing a
coronet, flying a kite outside a castle. The castle may well be meant to
represent Windsor and the boy a member of Queen Victoria's family.

CHILD'S MUG

Animals were a popular subject for 19th-century children's wares,
although many, like this scene, entitled The Little Jockey, of a child
astride a dog may be too sentimental for modern tastes. The mug has
copper lustre decoration on its rim, base and handle.

SPOON AND PUSHER

With the aim of teaching children how to feed themselves, these
silver utensils were designed so that the food could simply be
pushed on to the spoon. They were
often given as christening gifts.
This pair was made c.1900.

OTHER USEFUL TERMS

EGG-SHELL PORCELAIN An extremely thin translucent porcelain, which was originally produced in China in the early 18th century, but used by the Rozenburg factory in Holland during the Art Nouveau period.

GERMAN SILVER A method of electroplating in which a white alloy consisting of nickel, copper and zinc is used as a base metal. Unlike electroplating with a bright copper base metal, when the top layer of silver wears away, the white base metal is less noticeable.

SECESSIONIST MOVEMENT A trend favouring elongated, rectilinear forms, which began in Austria. The British designer Charles Rennie Mackintosh and the American designer Frank Lloyd Wright were both advocates of the movement.

DINNER SERVICE

The china, which is Austrian, is of a fairly traditional shape, although the serving dishes have a wavy outline. The influence of Art Nouveau here is restricted to the decoration, which incorporates the use of berries.

GLASS

The hock glasses are made of Bohemian glass and were produced by the Theresienthal works c.1904–10. The bowls have Art Nouveau decoration.

CUTLERY

The cutlery below is from a slightly earlier period. Although its design is not particularly Art Nouveau, it underlines the point that new cutlery services were not always purchased to update to a new style.

SERVING DISHES

The table service includes a covered tureen with handles and a lid (below), as well as an open vegetable dish (right) and an oval serving dish (opposite page).

SWEETMEAT DISH

This pewter sweetmeat dish (right) made by the WMF firm has a handle in the form of a nymph. Its shape is one that is commonly found in this style.

ART NOUVEAU

The Art Nouveau style emerged almost as an antidote to the eclectic styles of the 19th century. With its flowing forms, taken from nature, it was a style that favoured metal tablewares rather than ceramic ones.

The continuing growth of mass-production to meet the demand of the ever-growing middle classes was a feature of this age, although some firms, such as Liberty in London, produced wares that gave the impression of being hand-crafted. It was a period when the successful designers began to move away from producing items that

would be exclusively handmade for a wealthy client and instead created designs that could be machine-made for the wider public.

Art Nouveau designs fall into two categories. There are the flowing lines and forms of the French interpretation, which incorporate in their shape and decoration not only leaves, wood and flowers but also nymphs and dragonflies; and there is also the more linear approach, which was advocated by followers of the Secessionist Movement in Austria.

WINE BOTTLE HOLDER
The pewter wine bottle holder (below, left) made by the WMF firm is a classic example of how the swirling shapes and flowers of the design are suited to metalwork.

THE SETTING
The table setting became less elaborate than those typical of 19th-century tables. In this case, the cutlery is set for soup and the first and second courses, but there would have been fewer options to choose from compared to the number of dishes available beforehand.

CERAMICS

Art Nouveau, which takes its name from a Parisian shop, followed on from the ideas and precepts of the Arts and Crafts Movement. But instead of looking back to more traditional craftsmanship, it looked forward to new concepts that were to challenge the eclectic mainstream of 19th-century taste. It was a style that found advocates in continental Europe, Great Britain and the United States.

For their inspiration, artists drew on natural forms, such as plants, flowers and leaves, as well as on idealized female figures. They were also influenced by the Japanese style. These ideas were sometimes applied to both the form and the decoration of ornamental vases and elaborate bowls, such as those produced by the Royal Dux factory in Bohemia, whose wares often show Art Nouveau nymphs disporting themselves around the central bowl. This was not, however, always the case; with tablewares, for example, the influence of Art Nouveau was often restricted to the decoration.

Two manufacturers producing noteworthy wares were Rozenburg in Holland and Sèvres in France. Sèvres rose to the occasion not only with tablewares but also with biscuit figures. An example is the series of dancers with scarves, with their marvellous sense of rhythm and movement, known as *Le jeu de l'écharpe* ("the game of scarves"), which were designed by Agathon Léonard as a table decoration.

While pieces in Art Nouveau style continued to be made until the beginning of World War I, a new trend was already evident that would eventually flourish and become known as Art Deco in the mid-1920s. Function and form would replace decoration in importance.

ROZENBURG PORCELAIN

The Rozenburg factory was originally set up near The Hague in Holland to produce earthenware, but in 1899 it began to manufacture a very thin light porcelain, known as eggshell porcelain. These three pieces show some of their Art Nouveau shapes and decoration.

W.P. Hartgring has been credited with decorating this teapot in 1902.

Decoration on the teapot is closely allied to its shape, with the fish's lower fin following the angular shape of the spout.

The square-section box and cover with curved sides are painted with cartouches of lilylike flowers in Art Nouveau style.

The cover gracefully rises to form a curved integral handle.

The lid has a curved integral handle that is echoed in the shape of the fish's dorsal fin.

This piece, made in 1901, is attributed to the decorator J.L. Verhoog.

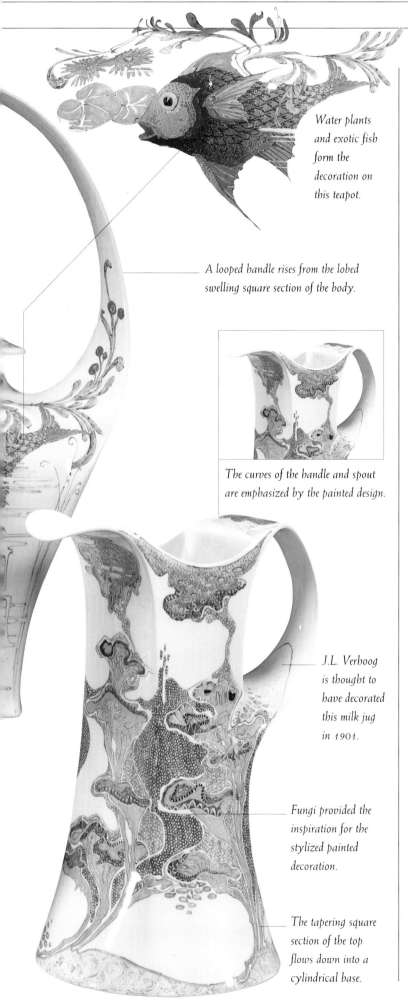

Water plants and exotic fish form the decoration on this teapot.

A looped handle rises from the lobed swelling square section of the body.

The curves of the handle and spout are emphasized by the painted design.

J.L. Verhoog is thought to have decorated this milk jug in 1901.

Fungi provided the inspiration for the stylized painted decoration.

The tapering square section of the top flows down into a cylindrical base.

TEA AND COFFEE SERVICE

Made by the Viennese porcelain manufacturer Josef Bock, c.1900, these pieces are part of a set designed by Jutta Sika at the Schule Koloman Moser. The forms, especially the wing-shaped handles with pierced holes, and the simple olive green circular motifs are a good example of her bold designs in the emerging modern style.

ROOKWOOD TEAPOT

The influence of Japanese ceramics can clearly be seen in the shape of this 1899 example of the useful wares produced by the well-known American Rookwood art pottery. Sallie Coyne, one of the artists who worked at the pottery, carried out the floral decoration in different coloured slips under the glaze.

LONGTON PORCELAIN TEAPOT

Influences from both Arts and Crafts and Art Nouveau are evident in this teapot and cover, dating from c.1910. Its chief attraction lies in the transfer-printed and enamelled suffragette badge on its side. This was designed by the leader of the British suffragettes, Mrs Pankhurst. Many examples of badgeware can be found, including tablewares from the great hotels and ship liners of the era.

METALWARE

There were two quite different approaches to Art Nouveau design: one was expressed in the sinuous lines, nymphs and flowers that are particularly associated with French designers, the other was the more linear style that was adopted by Charles Rennie Mackintosh and the Vienna Secessionists.

There was a demand by the wealthy for specially commissioned handmade pieces. At the same time, mass-produced goods in this new style were made and marketed by manufacturers for the less well-off. Pewter wares were suddenly popular again, because pewter was more affordable than silver, and so, too, were plated goods, such as those made by the German company Württemburgische Metallwarenfabrik.

No one could argue that the quality of the metalwares produced by the leading manufacturers was high, and the demand from the wealthy for high-quality silverware made by individual craftsmen in small workshops continued. Eventually, some of these craftsmen, such as the Dane Georg Jensen, gave up making wares by traditional methods to meet the demand for more wares.

Art Nouveau designs were easily applied to flatware forms, as is evident in those designed by Josef Hoffmann and Mackintosh and in the flamboyant curved shapes produced by Henry van de Velde and Richard Riemerschmid. In the United States, firms such as Tiffany and Gorham produced silverware in Art Nouveau designs.

SILVER-PLATED TEA AND COFFEE SERVICE

The German firm Württemburgische Metallwarenfabrik, more commonly referred to by the initials WMF, produced this set c. 1895. The factory is well known for its wares in the Art Nouveau style, using mass-production techniques.

The taller pot could be used to hold hot water for refilling the teapot when necessary, or as a coffee pot.

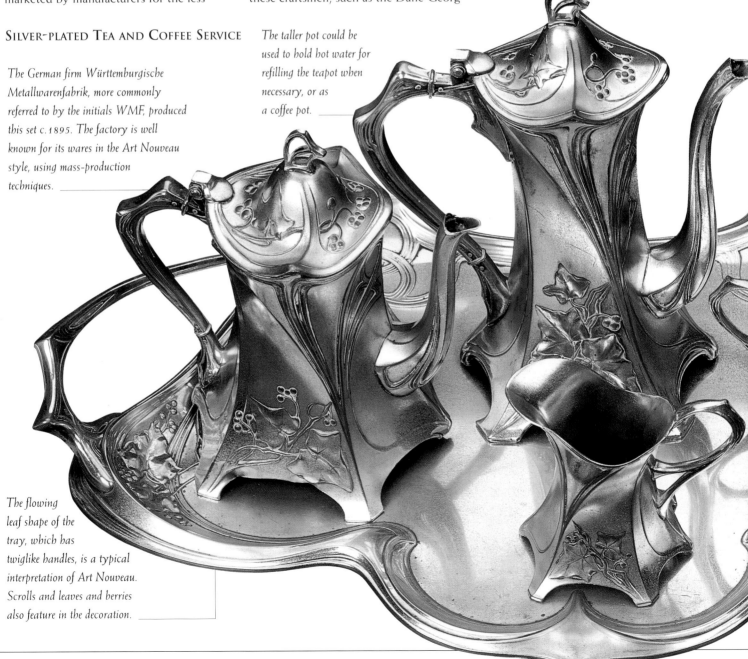

The flowing leaf shape of the tray, which has twiglike handles, is a typical interpretation of Art Nouveau. Scrolls and leaves and berries also feature in the decoration.

Like this sugar bowl, all the pieces on the tray rise from hexagonal bases into a swirling upper body, almost as if they have been given a strong twist during manufacture. This form is echoed in the lids of the two pots and the sugar bowl, all of which have exaggerated loop handles.

Both bodies and covers of all the pieces are decorated with curving lines and repoussé ivy leaves and berries.

SWEETMEAT DISH

This attractive dish has all the hallmarks of Art Nouveau design. Made of pewter, it reflects the renewed interest in pewter in this period. The sinuous curves of the leaves that make up the base of the dish are typical of the style, as is the handle in the form of a languorous nymph – who is designed to show off her own curves to the best advantage.

SILVERED-METAL WINE BOTTLE HOLDER

Produced by the German firm Württemburgische Metallwarenfabrik (WMF) c.1900, this pierced Art Nouveau bottle holder is made in what is known as German silver, or electroplated nickel silver, in which an alloy containing nickel is used. The shape is classic Art Nouveau, with interlaced curves emerging and re-emerging to form the type of pattern that gave the style its unmistakable look.

KAYSERZINN CANDELABRAS

This spectacular pair of candelabras, dating from c.1890, is an example of Kayserzinn pewter wares, which were produced by the Kayser factory in Germany. Although the overall impression of the Art Nouveau style is strong, the design is more restrained than usual. The candelabras have a flowing outline and the typical decorative motifs drawn from nature, but they do not have the excessive sinuous curves found on some pieces and, therefore, create a greater impact than might otherwise be expected.

LIBERTY

Shoppers in London's Regent Street will be familiar with the Liberty shop. This was not its original name – when Arthur Lasenby Liberty (later Sir Arthur) first opened his shop in 1875 it was known as East India House. The name aptly suited the Japanese and other Oriental wares that were part of the merchandise sold.

Liberty was influenced by some of the leading designers at the time such as E.W. Godwin, C.F.A. Voysey and Christopher Dresser. The shop soon became a flagship for new designs, at first for those of the Aesthetic Movement but, by the end of the 19th century, for Art Nouveau as well. The opening of a shop in Paris in 1889 brought Liberty's designs to continental Europe, and in Italy, to this day, the term *stile liberty* is applied to some Art Nouveau.

Much of the shop's products – which included fabrics for clothes and soft furnishings; ceramic and metal tablewares; and furniture – was made using industrial processes. By 1899, Liberty was selling a range of silverware under the brand name of Cymric. Many of these pieces were designed by Archibald Knox, among others, and made by the Birmingham silversmiths W.H. Haseler.

Knox came originally from the Isle of Man and was responsible for the Celtic-inspired designs found on much of the silver and pewter wares made for Liberty. He was influenced by the German Kayserzinn wares and, by 1903, Liberty was producing a similar range of goods in pewter under the brand name of Tudric.

Pottery was also an important part of the Liberty range of goods for the home, and leading art potters of the day supplied wares for the shop. Today, perhaps the best-known wares are those that were produced by William Moorcroft.

LIBERTY SILVER SPOONS

Most of these silver spoons were made in 1901–02. They show the high standard of design set by Liberty. Most have Celtic-inspired decoration. The name Cymric means Welsh.

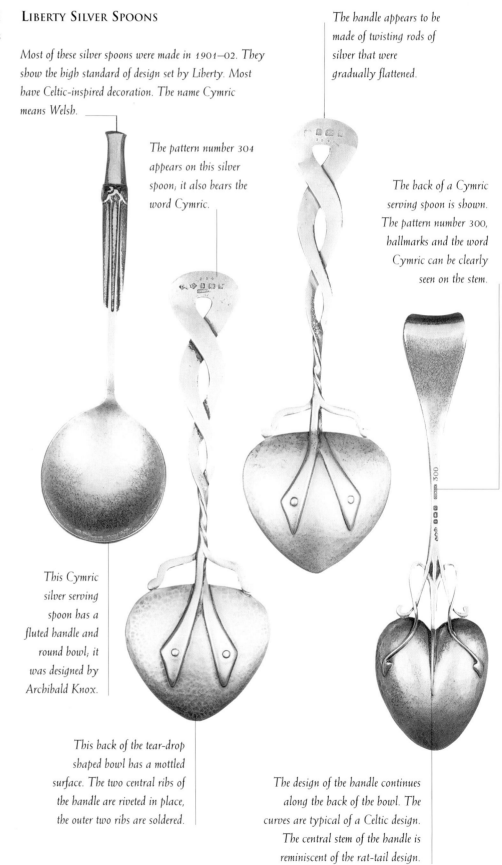

The pattern number 304 appears on this silver spoon; it also bears the word Cymric.

The handle appears to be made of twisting rods of silver that were gradually flattened.

The back of a Cymric serving spoon is shown. The pattern number 300, hallmarks and the word Cymric can be clearly seen on the stem.

This Cymric silver serving spoon has a fluted handle and round bowl; it was designed by Archibald Knox.

This back of the tear-drop shaped bowl has a mottled surface. The two central ribs of the handle are riveted in place, the outer two ribs are soldered.

The design of the handle continues along the back of the bowl. The curves are typical of a Celtic design. The central stem of the handle is reminiscent of the rat-tail design.

The front of the spoon with pattern number 300 shows how the handle gracefully bends over on top of itself and tapers to a scroll.

This Cymric enamelled spoon was made by Archibald Knox for the coronation of George V.

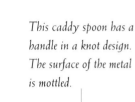

This caddy spoon has a handle in a knot design. The surface of the metal is mottled.

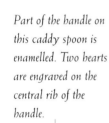

Part of the handle on this caddy spoon is enamelled. Two hearts are engraved on the central rib of the handle.

The knots are elements often associated with Celtic design.

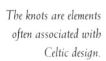

Archibald Knox designed this Cymric spoon for the coronation of Edward VII.

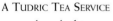

A TUDRIC TEA SERVICE

Although it was mass-produced, this pewter set designed by Archibald Knox has been hammered to give the impression that it has been handcrafted. The shape of the pieces shows some similarities to the designs being produced by the Guild of Handicraft, a group of designers who followed the ideas of William Morris. The wicker-bound handle on the teapot protected the user from the heat of the tea, which would have transferred to the metal.

MOORCROFT AND LIBERTY DISH

A rectangular Moorcroft plaque with a design of fruit was set into the base of this Tudric pewter dish, in what is not, visually, a particularly happy combination. The dish was made *c.*1908. Most Tudric ware carries the name somewhere on the piece and it may have a shape number as well.

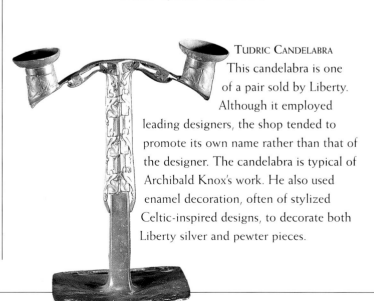

TUDRIC CANDELABRA

This candelabra is one of a pair sold by Liberty. Although it employed leading designers, the shop tended to promote its own name rather than that of the designer. The candelabra is typical of Archibald Knox's work. He also used enamel decoration, often of stylized Celtic-inspired designs, to decorate both Liberty silver and pewter pieces.

ART NOUVEAU DESIGNERS

The growth and development of any style depends on the designers who first introduce it and on those who follow their example. There were two differing approaches to Art Nouveau, both with a common goal: to replace the previous vogue for revivals with some new concept. The French designers, such as René Lalique and those in the École de Nancy, advocated the use of natural forms such as trees and flowers. Together with other designers, such as the Belgians Victor Horta and Henry van de Velde and the American Louis C. Tiffany, they promoted this style.

In Austria, the Secessionist Movement, perhaps best typified by the Wiener Werkstätte – an Austrian association of artists and craftsmen founded in 1903 – favoured the more elongated, rectilinear forms that were advocated by Charles Rennie Mackintosh, who was probably the only real British exponent of this new art. In the United States, the architect and designer Frank Lloyd Wright followed this trend as well.

The word "designer" seems almost automatically to apply to someone working in a small workshop, handcrafting individual items for the wealthier members of society. While this was sometimes true in the Art Nouveau period, there were those who designed for a wider audience by working for manufacturers. In fact, it is not unusual on tablewares of this date to find not only the manufacturer's marks but also a mark denoting the particular retailer for whom the piece was made.

LIQUEUR SET

An example of German Art Nouveau, this white metal and glass set was designed c.1900 by the German architect and designer Patriz Huber. It consists of a liqueur decanter and six glasses in cup-shaped frames.

The elongated shape of the jug and the linear supports and rectangular feet are representative of the Secessionist Movement.

Huber's silver designs were executed by the firm of Martin Mayer in Mainz.

The finial on the cover is in the shape of an egglike knob supported by four bracket-shaped feet.

Because the spout is covered, the lid has to be raised, using the thumbpiece opposite the spout, to pour out the liquid.

The metal frames holding the glasses have vertical supports that rise to end in stylized foliate "capitals". The metal frame of the jug has similar supports.

White metal was used to make the frames. The term can be applied either to Britannia Metal (see pp.84–85) or to silver that does not fulfil the British hallmarking requirements, as is the case here.

SET OF EARTHENWARE PLATES

Designed by one of the leading French exponents of Art Nouveau, Émile Gallé, these plates were supplied to Bailey-Bank & Biddle's department store in Philadelphia *c*.1897. The moulded plates were tin-glazed in the traditional faience method and hand-painted in the typical, free-flowing style that Gallé favoured. On some of his earthenwares, Gallé created an iridescent effect by applying a mixture that included precious metals before glazing.

ELECTROPLATED METAL SPOON WARMER

An unusual object, this spoon warmer was made by the Birmingham firm of Hukin and Heath, which made many of the pieces designed by Dr Christopher Dresser. Although not directly attributed to him, the design shows many of the elements found in his work, such as the four spiky feet and the angular handle with its bar of ebonized wood. Hot water was poured into the container's base through the capped opening on the right. Spoons were then inserted through the opening on the left to warm them before eating ice cream and other foods.

SILVER SPOONS AND FORKS

These spoons and forks were made in 1902 by A.D.W. Hislop, following a design by Charles R. Mackintosh, who relied on wealthy patronage. They are part of a set commissioned for the head of the Glasgow School of Art. The long, tapering stems are pierced with pointed ovals, a motif often found in Mackintosh's work. The overall design, with its fluid lines, anticipates the emergence of Art Deco.

OTHER USEFUL TERMS

ABSTRACTION A trend started in Germany and Russia in which emphasis was placed on the form and function of a piece, not the decoration. The most notable followers of this trend were designers influenced by the Bauhaus movement.

BAUHAUS MOVEMENT An approach to design, led by the German Walter Gropius, which emphasized simplicity in design.

STAMFORD SHAPE Designed by the Frenchman Jean Tetard, a D-like shape used for the body of silver and ceramic wares.

UREA FORMALDEHYDE A type of plastic that was developed in 1928, it was popular for producing tablewares – especially in the United States – because of its durability.

THE MEAL

Afternoon tea was a meal that could be enjoyed in the sitting room, using a plethora of small occasional tables, or it could be taken more formally at the dining table, as here. Other items on the table would include serving platters for sandwiches, scones and biscuits.

TEA SERVICE

The tea set, which includes a milk jug, teapot and sugar bowl, has a colourful pattern which was typical of china used in this period. The pattern is also found on the front of the cups. More affluent households may have used a silver teapot, milk jug and sugar bowl.

CAKE STAND

The cake rests on a cake stand of moulded glass. Smaller individual cakes were often served, too; they would have been on a separate serving platter.

ART DECO

W orld War I changed society for ever, and those who had managed to survive it wanted to forget the old order. This resulted in a new era, which is often referred to as the Jazz Age. The mood of this new age led to a new decorative style, which became known as Art Deco, and it frequently featured colourful geometric or abstract patterns.

Methods of travel grew ever faster during the 1920s and '30s and this is reflected in the novelty wares of the day, with teapots, for example, sometimes shaped like ships, cars and planes. The expansion of the American film industry, especially after the first "talkies" came out in 1927, meant that people could see this new decorative style on the big screen, and they sought to copy it at home. Although the majority of people could not afford to redecorate their houses in the new taste, many of them could afford to buy a mass-produced tea or dinner set in the new style.

The making of specially designed china for children continued to thrive, but now decoration included characters from Walt Disney cartoons and children's storybooks. Plastics were also developed during this period and were used to make many domestic objects, including those found on the dining-room table.

THE SETTING
The place setting for afternoon tea has a larger plate for sandwiches, cakes and scones and a smaller plate for biscuits.

CUTLERY
The knife would be used to split the scones before spreading them with jam and, perhaps, topping them with clotted cream. The fork was used to eat cake and the spoon for stirring a cup of tea.

ABSTRACTION AND GEOMETRY

Just as there had been differing expressions of Art Nouveau, so were there different conceptions of the style known as Art Deco, which emerged in the 1920s and 1930s. It reflected the changes in a society that had survived the horrors of World War I and now wanted to enjoy the peace that brought in the Roaring Twenties.

The style promoted by French designers at the 1925 Exposition Internationale des Art Décoratifs et Industriels Modernes in Paris was in some ways traditional, perhaps because some of these designs were a modern interpretation of the Louis XVI and Directoire styles. But influences were also evident from South American Aztec architecture and from Africa, in particular Egypt, where the discovery of Tutankhamun's tomb in 1922 had aroused great interest. One feature derived from these various sources was the use of geometric ornament; although the world of flora and fauna was not ignored, such designs were often highly stylized.

Another element in Art Deco design was abstraction, which found its roots in Germany and Russia. The proponents of Abstraction placed an emphasis on form and function rather than ornamentation; they also believed that items should be made by mechanical processes, using the most advanced materials, so that they could reach the mass market rather than just the wealthy few. The most notable German designers were part of the Bauhaus movement (see pp.132–133), some of whose members were influenced by the new Russian look that had emerged since the 1917 revolution.

These influences spread across the Atlantic to the United States, where the various types of decoration and design were adopted with success.

WINDBELLS PATTERN TEA SET

This tea set was designed by Clarice Cliff and made at the Newport factory, where she worked from 1927.

Bright colours are typical of Cliff's work, and her assistants would have painted these pieces by hand. Reproductions of Cliff's wares are usually more subdued than the originals.

The cups, with their triangular handles, are an example of Cliff's use of conical shapes. The rims of the saucers flare up, echoing this form.

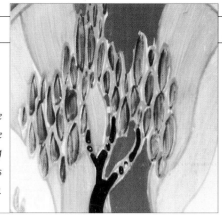

The Windbells pattern on these pieces is reminiscent of textile designs of the period, reflecting the fact that Clarice Cliff was also a fabric designer.

SUGAR SIFTER

The body of this geometric silver sifter, produced in Birmingham in 1935, is composed of triangles that are echoed in the top, which is pierced to allow the sugar to be shaken out. Although the influence of Art Deco is clearly shown in the sifter's shape, the machine-turned decoration is more traditional.

Cliff copied the D-like Stamford shape from a silver tea set designed by the Frenchman Jean Tetard for his family firm. The only major difference between the designs is that the china teapot does not have the solid handle of the original model.

OVAL DISH

This is an example of 1920s Russian porcelain decorated with a design by K. Mareburg. The colours and shapes in the design reflect the geometric Suprematist forms that were popular in Russia at the time and which influenced some Western designers. The Russian factories also produced wares decorated with images and slogans that were inspired by the Revolution.

"CUBIST" PATTERN PLATE

The influence of Modernism can clearly be seen in this highly colourful design by Susie Cooper, which combines geometric forms with abstract shapes. The fairly strong colours used on this plate, which was made c.1928, were among those favoured by Susie Cooper at this time. She only decorated wares in this way for a few years before moving on to the banded decoration for which she is better known.

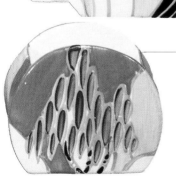

The sugar bowl and milk jug are in the same Stamford shape as the teapot.

ART DECO DESIGNS

There were several strands of the Art Deco style working together during its earlier period in the 1920s, but the changing economic and political climate in the 1930s brought about a more modernistic look. The French silversmith Jean Puiforçat, who favoured the modernistic approach in his silver designs, encapsulated the French taste of the 1920s and '30s. Jean Luce was a French ceramics designer who also created wares in the Art Deco style.

At the same time, the idea of designers working specifically for the mass-production market became more firmly established. Indeed, this was one of the stated objectives of the Bauhaus, a school established by the German Walter Gropius in 1919. Although it was in existence for only a short time, the influence of the

Bauhaus movement, and especially of Walter Gropius, was immense. Not only was art education influenced, but the whole development of art and architecture during the 20th century owes a debt to the ideals of the movement.

Supporters of the Bauhaus movement believed that skills, not art, could be taught and that students should be trained in workshops in a variety of media – including ceramics, woodwork, metalwork and textiles. There was also an emphasis on designing prototypes that could be mass-produced. The school taught geometry, design and construction, and it stressed the importance of designing with a simplicity of style and in forms that would clearly indicate the purpose for which an object had been designed.

However, the rise of Fascism and Adolf Hitler meant that, in accordance with the Nazi Party's cultural policy, the school was closed in 1933 to rid the country of "decadent" and Bolshevistic art. Some leading designers, such as Trude Petri – who was well known for her ceramic designs – continued to work in the changed political climate, while others, including Walter Gropius, decided to flee to the United States, taking with them their Bauhaus ideals.

The German Otto Lindig, who was an advocate of mass production, is just one of the designers who have created wares which clearly reflect an association with the Bauhaus movement. The shapes of his wares are strong and practical and the only decoration is in the glazes.

SILVER-GILT BOWL

This bowl, made in 1935, is an excursion into Art Deco by the designer Omar Ramsden. It is in the form of two classically attired maidens stretching a cloth between them. The women serve as handles for the bowl and as legs.

The silver is covered with gilding to protect the piece from corrosive chemicals found in certain foods.

A feature of many Art Deco female figures is their vigorous, athletic appearance, which is clearly evident here.

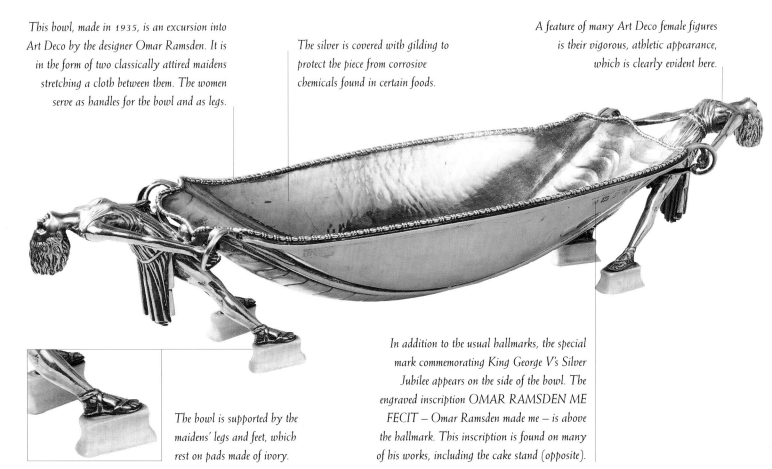

The bowl is supported by the maidens' legs and feet, which rest on pads made of ivory.

In addition to the usual hallmarks, the special mark commemorating King George V's Silver Jubilee appears on the side of the bowl. The engraved inscription OMAR RAMSDEN ME FECIT – Omar Ramsden made me – is above the hallmark. This inscription is found on many of his works, including the cake stand (opposite).

CAKE STAND

Despite its date of manufacture, this cake stand, made by Omar Ramsden in 1932, still shows the influence of Art Nouveau in its design, although there are also elements of Art Deco. Ramsden is well known for silverwares in both the Art Nouveau and Arts and Crafts styles, as well as making pieces in revival styles.

Graceful snowdrops and foliage form the handle.

Brackets on the frame hold the plates in place.

The openwork silver frame, which resembles a bee skep, stands on four scroll and bun feet.

The stand would have been used during afternoon tea, with cakes being served on the three plates of graduated size.

TEA SERVICE

Made by the Belgian firm of Delheide c.1930, this tea service is silver plated. The flowing, curving shapes are typical of some of their wares of the period, as are the shaped ivory handles; ivory was a popular material at this time. The shape of the tray echoes that of the tea set. It is the shape of these pieces that categorize them as Art Deco.

PITCHERS AND A CHOCOLATE POT

This group of wares was designed by Otto Lindig and produced between 1920 and 1923. The chocolate pot on the right is a terracotta prototype for a design that was intended for mass production, however, it was never manufactured as a series. The two pitchers were made of stoneware and glazed, and the smaller one displays a slight iridescence.

TAZZA

When designing silver pieces – especially his earlier ones – Jean Puiforçat often used contrasting materials, such as wood, ivory or semiprecious stones, to provide a decorative element. This elegant tazza, made in Puiforçat's workshops in the 1920s, is a combination of silver plate and wood – the tazza's silver-plate bowl is supported by eight wooden uprights on a low silver-plate base.

BREAKFAST WARES

By the 1930s, the concept of breakfast had changed. Gone were the several hot and cold courses enjoyed on a daily basis in Victorian and Edwardian times – for most people, breakfast had become a casual affair.

The idea of having cereal at breakfast had become more fashionable, with porridge and processed cereals, such as Shredded Wheat and cornflakes, becoming an acceptable part of the morning diet. Bacon and eggs were still popular, as was toast with butter and marmalade or some other sort of preserve or honey.

Special breakfast sets were now made – sometimes for only one or two people – with all the components matching, including the teapot and toast rack. And sometimes the set included a tray for those lucky enough to be served breakfast in bed. Children were not forgotten, for special breakfast sets were also made for them.

Not all breakfast wares were made from ceramics or metal. Plastics, although first introduced in the 19th century, were now increasingly popular – especially in the United States, where firms such as Bakelite and Catlin were using this material to manufacture a variety of tablewares, as well as numerous other objects, including radios and hairdryers. Colour was a big selling point for this new product, and plates, egg cups, cruets, beakers and cups and saucers were all made in bright hues and with a variety of decorative effects.

SUSIE COOPER BREAKFAST SET

Decorated at the Susie Cooper Crown Works c.1937, this breakfast set for one is an example of her Kestrel design shape. It features a cereal bowl, plate, cup and saucer, teapot, hot-water jug, milk jug and sugar bowl, as well as a toast rack – everything that would be needed for the breakfast table or tray.

The streamlined handles on the lid are placed slightly off-centre. They are white, as are the handles on the bodies of the pots and milk jug.

The cereal bowl was a new addition to tableware. It was not until the early 20th century that Dr John Harvey Kellogg popularized cereal – first with crisp flakes of wheat, which were soon followed by cornflakes.

White glaze outlines the rim of the milk jug and hot-water pot, as well as the spout. The interiors of these pieces, along with the sugar bowl and cups, were left in the white glaze.

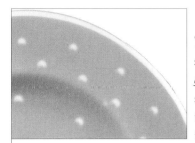

The salmon-pink ground colour was sprayed on top of a white background glaze. The white dots were created by scratching off areas of colour to reveal the glaze below before the piece was fired; this technique is known as sgraffito.

This set is salmon pink in colour, with an overall design of white spots. Sets were also made in lime yellow, blue and turquoise – these colours reflected Cooper's move toward using more restful colours than those seen in her earlier cubist designs.

Similar polka-dot wares were supplied by Susie Cooper to the John Lewis department store, but on these wares, the polka dots were applied to the basic ground colour.

The set was designed for one person, as is evident in the toast rack, which can hold only two slices of toast.

JAM CRUET
The Chase firm made this cruet, which is a good example of American chrome from the 1930s. The cruet could be used for serving two different types of preserve or relish. Its simple, practical shape is typical of those products that would have been just as much at home in a domestic kitchen as in a roadside diner.

UREA FORMALDEHYDE TOAST RACK
This marbled toast rack, which was made in the 1930s, is not marked, but it is probably of British manufacture. It is an example of the new pale-colour plastic wares that were being made for use in the home. Its practical size and the durable nature of the material have guaranteed its continued use.

HONEY BOX
Made in the mid-1920s, this honey box is an example of Poole Pottery from the firm set up as Carter Stabler Adams in 1921. The colour and square shape are typical of the Art Deco style. The box was used to hold a honeycomb, as is indicated by the handle in the shape of a bee among flowers. The factory also made the standard round pots.

NOVELTY WARES

The proliferation of firms producing ceramics in the early 20th century meant that they had to compete even harder to persuade people to buy their wares. One area that caught the buying public's imagination was novelty wares. These ranged from obvious candidates for this treatment, such as salts and peppers, to sophisticated items such as knife rests.

The teapot was a favourite upon which the designer could let his or her imagination run free. Several firms made teapots that were far more entertaining than the octagonal, hexagonal and cube shapes that were among those manufactured in the 1920s. Cars, cottages, cartoon characters, footballs and even the ubiquitous Scottie dog were now part of a growing range of teapots available, and some of them were accompanied by matching sugar bowls and milk jugs.

Many firms, including John Beswick, Carlton Ware, Crown Devon and Grimwades, produced embossed salad wares, with dishes and bowls in the shape of leaves. Cruet sets, preserve pots and cheese dishes are some of the many other pieces made in novelty shapes. Special wares for children had already been made (see pp.116–117), but by this time the designs were numerous and novel.

For those wanting to eat in the garden a new combination of plate and saucer was "reinvented". This was known as a tennis, or croquet, set: the plate was often racquet-shaped, tapering to a narrow end where there was a recess in which a cup could be placed as if in a saucer. In the 1950s the set appeared in the form of a television.

SHELLEY TOADSTOOL TEAPOT
This teapot was designed by the children's story illustrator Mabel Lucie Attwell for Shelley Potteries. A gnome, who lives in the toadstool house, stands at the open door.

LEIGHTON NURSERY TEAPOT
Designed by Bourne and Leigh Leighton, this teapot has a handle and spout in the shape of a branch. The body is decorated with an elf sitting among toadstools.

STAFFORDSHIRE WAGON TRAIN TEA SET
The Wild West is evoked in this set. The larger wagon is the teapot and is followed by a smaller milk jug wagon and a sugar bowl wagon. A teapot in the form of a car, with a sugar bowl as a hook-on trailer, was made by Sadler.

WILKINSON TEAPOT

This teapot in the form of a circus clown was made from a design by the artist Dame Laura Knight – who mainly painted circus and ballet themes – in collaboration with the designer Clarice Cliff in 1934. The pot, part of a tableware range, was never mass-produced, so it is rare.

MILK JUG BY SHELLEY

This rabbit milk jug was part of a set designed by Mabel Lucie Attwell for Shelley. The teapot was a duck and the sugar bowl a chicken.

DONALD DUCK TEAPOT

Cartoon characters were a popular subject for nursery wares, and this Donald Duck teapot was produced by Wade, Heath and Co. in various sizes and colours. They also made wares inspired by *Snow White and the Seven Dwarfs* and Mickey Mouse. Paragon china also made Mickey Mouse wares, after securing the rights from Walt Disney.

GALLIA KNIFE RESTS

These knife rests, from a set of six, were made by the French firm of Christofle, which is renowned for its silver-plated wares. They were made of gallia, a type of plating introduced by Christofle in 1900. The rests are examples of the more sophisticated novelty wares and would have been used with knives. They are still reproduced and are now also used as chopstick rests.

NOVELTY CRUETS

The red pepper in this set on a leaf-shaped tray appropriately holds the pepper; a green pea pod is for the salt. Novelty cruets were extremely popular and were made in a variety of food shapes, including fruits and even lamb chops. The range of subjects was endless: another example is this one in the shape of an ocean liner. The funnels and smoke form the handle of a central mustard pot, and containers fore and aft hold the pepper and salt. Today, many less-expensive novelty cruets are available to the collector.

NAPKIN RINGS

Made by the Royal Doulton factory, which was also renowned for its Bunnykins wares designed by Barbara Vernon, these napkin rings are surmounted by characters from Charles Dickens's *Pickwick Papers*. Other firms also made napkin rings in various novel shapes.

OTHER USEFUL TERMS

LITHOGRAPHY A printing technique in which a crayon is used to draw the pattern on a hard flat surface such as a metal plate. Water and ink are poured over the surface; the crayon retains the ink but repels the water. The ink is then transferred to the ware, using pressure.

MIX AND MATCH WARES A colour-driven trend, in which individual pieces could be purchased with the idea of mixing together items in a variety of colours. If preferred, of course, the pieces could be of one colour.

STREAMLINING A style led by the modernist movement in which there was an absence of ornament and an emphasis on horizontal lines.

DINNER SERVICE

The table is set with part of a Wedgwood service designed by Eric Ravilious in 1939. World War II prevented this set from being produced until the early 1950s, however, the subject and design are very typical of the 1930s and '40s. The pieces from the service shown here are dinner and side plates, together with a serving plate and a sauce boat and stand.

THE PATTERN

The pieces were decorated with different travel scenes: the main plate has a scene with a sailing boat; the large platter shows a train. The patterns were applied by the lithography process, of which Ravilious was a pioneer.

CUTLERY

The silver-plated cutlery is Scandinavian and was designed by the Swedish designer Sigvard Bernadotte in 1939. Scandinavian flatwares enjoy a high reputation for the simplicity and elegance of their design. The table is set for soup, first and second courses.

THE MASS MARKET

By the 1930s, the mass market had truly arrived and was catered for by the manufacturers of ceramic and metal tablewares in the popular styles of the day. As the Western world began to recover from the Great Depression, there was a move toward patterns more simple than those found in the previous decade.

The United States was now influential in the field of design and it was there that the colourful mix and match wares became popular. The concept soon crossed the Atlantic to Great Britain and Europe, although it was not always so colourfully reinterpreted. The fascination with speed still caught the public's imagination and was often reflected in the shape of a variety of objects, including tableware.

In an effort to recover from the costs of World War II, many countries experienced a period of austerity. In Great Britain, cutting costs meant that patterns were not allowed on tablewares, unless they were made for export.

GLASSES
The wine glasses and water tumblers are examples of Scandinavian glass and represent the high quality of glasswares manufactured there at that time and in later decades.

THE SETTING
During the 1930s and 40s the move toward greater informality became more evident. A sense of this can be drawn from this setting, for example, the wine bottle stands on the table rather than in a cooler or bottle holder. All the different elements have a lighter, less formal appearance than earlier examples.

STREAMLINING

The economic climate in the United States and Europe had worsened in the wake of the Wall Street Crash of 1929, which led to the Great Depression. In this era society had to become more responsible, and there was a move away from the more decorative aspects of the French-style Art Deco toward the more modernistic and practical approach advocated by designers of the Bauhaus movement (see pp.132–33). The design of tableware became less flamboyant.

One of the great passions of the decade was speed, whether on land, sea or in the air. This fascination manifested itself in the streamlined designs produced by the modernists. There was an absence of ornament and a concentration on horizontal lines rather than vertical ones, and on curves rather than angular shapes. This new form echoed the teardrop shapes found in the various forms of transportation, including the bodies of cars, such as the Bugatti; aircraft, such as the Hindenburg; and ships, such as the Queen Mary.

American influence had by this time also become more predominant; in particular, it was established through the popularity of American films, in which contemporary interiors could be seen by viewers not only in the United States but also in Europe. Designers now aimed their wares at all levels of the market so that everyone could live in a modern style, or at least incorporate some elements of it into their homes. Indeed, despite – or perhaps as a result of – the Depression, the new style of streamlining was widely promoted in the hopes of stimulating production and thereby increasing employment.

SILVER TEA SET

The semicircular finial of the teapot and the handle are made of wood.

Harold Stabler designed this tea set in the early 1930s. He was a designer of jewellery and silver tablewares and, in 1921, co-founded the Poole Pottery, which continues to operate to this day.

Adie Brothers Ltd manufactured the set, which has a Birmingham hallmark for 1934.

The stepped outline of the teapot lid is also found in many other areas of Art Deco design, including architecture.

Many designers used clean geometric shapes, an example of which can be seen in the handles of both the teapot and the milk jug.

The handle is made of wood; as has been the case for hundreds of years, the material provided insulation against the heat transferred to the metal of the pot from the hot beverage.

TEAPOT, CUP AND SAUCER

The shape of these pieces from a pottery tea set by Margaret Heyman-Marks clearly shows her Bauhaus training. The set is a good example of the functional streamlined shapes advocated by the Bauhaus designers in the 1920s, which were copied so widely in the 1930s. The round discs serve as handles; the lid of the teapot and its spout are designed to appear to be an integral part of the pot's body.

The pieces are supported by stepped feet. The central foot on the teapot, which is 20 cm (8 inches) long, is for decorative purposes.

COFFEE POT

This 1930s ceramic example of the English interpretation of streamlining was designed by Susie Cooper. Here the streamlining effect is confined to the spout and the handle on the lid. The curves of the pattern also give an impression of movement.

A simplicity of design, which emphasized a reliance on line and the absence of decoration, was a feature of many pieces made in the 1930s. It reflected the contemporary interest in streamlining, which was inspired by the exciting increases in speed being achieved both on land and in the air.

SILVER EWER

The interest in streamlining continued after the end of World War II, as can be seen in this Scandinavian ewer, which was produced *c.*1952. It was designed by Henning Koppel for the Danish firm of Georg Jensen. The flowing lines of streamlining are accentuated on the ewer with the more pronounced curve of its low-centred body.

Stabler had his own workshop at one time but later designed for firms. He designed sets like this one in silver and silver plate, but also made similar items in stainless steel for the Sheffield firm of Firth Vicken.

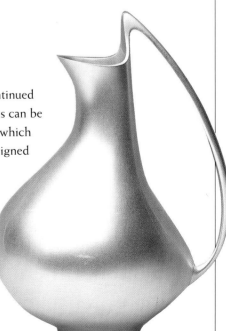

MIX AND MATCH WARES

In the United States, the idea of colour in the home was promoted by the manufacturers of ceramics who designed a range of wares that could be bought cheaply in retail outlets, including Woolworths. This trend started first on the West Coast, but it soon moved to the eastern states, too.

Perhaps the best known of these wares is the Fiesta range, which was designed by the British-born Frederick Hurten Rhead and marketed in the latter part of the 1930s. The range covered wares for everything from the preparation of food to its presentation at the table. Although the shapes and decoration were kept to a minimum, this was more than compensated for by the daring use of colour. The five original colours were ivory, blue, green, yellow and red.

Rhead designed the pieces with the intention that they should be mixed in use, which emphasized the informality in eating during the time – a practice that was also advocated by the American designer Russel Wright (see the main piece). Woolworths marketed the Harlequin range of wares, which could also be mixed and matched, and it was even more inexpensive than the Fiesta range – although both were manufactured by the Homer Laughlin China Company of East Liverpool, Ohio.

In England, the idea of mix and match wares was also gaining popularity, and the Poole Pottery produced a range of twin-tone wares, in which pastel colours were used. There was a certain British reserve in the use of colours when compared with the vibrant, warm tones of their American counterparts.

AMERICAN TABLEWARES

Russel Wright, who designed these pieces, firmly believed that the public should be able to purchase well-designed wares at reasonable prices.

The spout is designed as part of the body of the jug.

The jug and bowl are examples of Wright's American Modern tableware. Although designed in 1937, it was not made until 1939 by the Steubenville Pottery. Over the following 20 years, about 80 million pieces were sold.

The flowing, tapering shape of the water jug is a distinctive element of Wright's design.

As the two different ranges shown here demonstrate, the pieces in different colours could be used together to create an informal mood. The colours included Coral, Granite Grey, Bean Brown, Seafoam Blue, Chartreuse, Curry and White.

This vegetable dish is an example of the Casual China range designed by Russel Wright.

SUNDAE DISHES

These dishes are of the type that could have been purchased at Woolworths; they are made from moulded glass and date from the 1950s. Their bright colours were inspired by Fiesta wares, and the use of glass reflects the growing use of non-ceramic materials for tablewares.

SOUP BOWL AND STAND

Poole Pottery made this bowl and stand in the 1950s. The shape of the pieces and the twin-tone colouring had been introduced by Poole before World War II and its popularity continued; in fact, there were more than two dozen different colour combinations. Many of the earlier 1930s examples were in their Streamline range.

CARNIVAL TEA CUPS AND SAUCERS

Made by Johnson Bros, which later became part of the Wedgwood Group, these cups and saucers show the colour combinations possible with these wares. Some people preferred sets in only one colour, but others were free to mix the pieces, which were sold individually. The tapering design of the cups indicate their 1950s' origin.

The theory behind this tableware was that pieces could be added to a "set" as required: the components and quantities were determined by the owner.

The bowl has an organic shape found in many of the pieces designed by Russel Wright.

Instead of a normal handle, the lid of the dish has two shaped dimples with a central grip by which the lid can be lifted. (The detail shows the underside of the lid.)

SCANDINAVIAN WARES

The designers in Scandinavia typically tried to incorporate traditional local design elements into all their wares, even the modern-looking pieces. It was not until the 1930s, with the introduction of ideas from the Bauhaus movement (see pp.132–33), that the designers changed to an even more simple, undecorated style.

Some of these Scandinavian designers had lengthy careers, starting before World War II, and by the 1950s, the quality of their work placed them among the main trendsetters. For example, the clean, simple lines and organic shapes first promoted by Alvar Aalto in the 1920s and '30s and the tableware produced to Wilhelm Kage's designs at the Swedish Gustavsberg factory were reaching a larger audience. At the same time, the Scandinavian ceramics factories, although using mass-production techniques, also encouraged their designers to produce experimental one-off pieces.

In the 1950s, the Finnish Arabia factory produced mix and match wares similar to those found in the United States, Great Britain and elsewhere in Europe. Sweden had been a neutral country during World War II and, during that time, it had become one of the leaders in the production of ceramics. Its factories of Rorstrand and Gustavsberg produced several different types of tablewares both in china and earthenware, among them the highly patterned wares designed by Marianne Westman and the strongly textured surfaces of Hertha Bengtson's Blue Fire design.

FLATWARE SERVICE

This service was made by the Danish firm of Georg Jensen, following a 1915 design by Johan Rohde. It is known as the Acorn pattern – or the King's pattern in Denmark – and is still made today.

The two-tined fork is for serving meat.

The knife with the pointed blade is a fish knife.

The scrolling decoration at the top of the forks and spoons complements the finials.

These tongs are for serving sugar.

This ladle is used to serve soup.

The salt cellars are lined with blue glass. The tiny spoon to the left of the cake server is used to remove salt from the cellar.

Sometimes this piece is mistaken for a fish slice, but it is actually a cake server.

More than 200 pieces are manufactured in this
popular pattern. Along with the standard knives, forks
and spoons are a variety of serving utensils, including
ladles, salt cellars, salad servers and sugar tongs.

VEGETABLE DISH AND A PAIR OF CANDELABRAS
The vegetable dish was designed in 1928 for the firm of Georg
Jensen by Harald Nielsen, while the candelabras, manufactured
c.1920, were designed by Bjarne Weimar. The decoration on both
the dish and the candelabras consists of stylized foliage, which was a
feature frequently found on Scandinavian pieces at this time. The
dish is decorated with berries as well.

The soup spoon
has a fairly
deep, rounded
bowl.

The short knife with the
wide curved blade is a
butter knife.

Smaller than the
soup ladle, this
one would be
used to serve
a sauce.

The fluted stems and the
styling of the acorn finial
clearly indicate that in this
design Rohde was inspired
by classical motifs.

FARSTA STUDIO O BOWL
Wilhelm Kage designed this bowl for the Gustavsberg factory in
1957, almost at the end of his long association with the company.
Over the years he designed many items of tableware for the factory,
but by this time was producing only studio pieces for individual sales.
This piece is from the Farsta series and reflects Kage's continuing
interest in form and textured surfaces.

STONEWARE TEAPOT AND JUG
An example of 1950s
stacking wares, this
combination of a teapot
sitting on top of a jug was
designed for the
Rorstrand factory by
Gunnar Nylund, the
factory's artistic
director. His wares
are almost always of
organic form, with
simple curved lines.
Nylund was also known
for designing glassware.

A FOCUS ON THE TOP 10 PATTERNS

It is difficult to say what makes a pattern enduringly popular. The Oriental style, obvious in the Imari pattern, is discernible also in the blue and white examples, which were influenced by the early Chinese blue and white wares. Flowers seem to predominate in most patterns – figures are confined to the Spode Blue Italian and the Willow patterns.

The designs shown here have a proven track record. Most of the older ones are still produced today – even if not by the original factory – and the newer ones have become classics overnight. No doubt they will all still be sought for years to come.

Imari

The pattern is named after the Japanese port from which Arita porcelain was shipped at the end of the 17th century. The decoration, which was based on contemporary textiles, is divided into panels and features iron-red, underglaze blue and gilding, sometimes with other colours. The decoration was, and still is, copied in Europe; Coalport made these pieces.

Old Country Roses

Although it was only made in 1962, this pattern designed by Harold Holdcroft has become one of the most popular patterns. Various tablewares and ornaments have been produced in this colourful, traditional pattern to meet public demand. It is made in England by Royal Albert China, which is part of the Royal Doulton Group.

Napoleon Ivy

This simple border of ivy leaves upon creamware was made by Wedgwood in 1815. Napoleon is believed to have used a service in this pattern while in exile, but there is no documentary proof.

Feuille de choux

This is the name given to the pattern with raised borders found on Sèvres wares. It resembles the edge of a cabbage leaf (its name is the French for cabbage) and is usually painted with a colour and some gilding. *Feuille de choux* was used extensively at Sèvres during the 18th century and was copied by British and other European factories.

Haddon Hall

One of the Minton firm's most popular patterns, Haddon Hall was designed by John Wadsworth in 1948. It is derived from wall paintings, needlework and tapestries at Haddon Hall in Derbyshire.

Spode Blue Italian

This famous 1816 blue and white design is thought to be based on an as yet unidentified old master painting. Recent research suggests that the scene is a pastiche, since the ruins on the left are similar to the Great Baths at Tivoli, while the houses are similar to those found in Umbria and the castle resembles those found in the Piedmont region.

Onion Pattern

When this pattern, based on a Chinese design, was first interpreted at the Meissen factory in the 18th century, it was called the Onion pattern because the painters mistook the Chinese design of peaches with leaves and flowers for one featuring onions. It was also copied by other European factories.

Flora Danica

This pattern, known as Flora Danica, or Danish Flowers, was taken from folios in the royal library in Copenhagen. In 1790, the future King Frederick VI of Denmark ordered a service with the pattern, originally as a gift for Catherine the Great of Russia. However, she died before the service was completed in 1802, so it became the property of the king – he first used it on his birthday, 29 January 1803.

Angoulême sprig

Also known as the Chantilly sprig – it was first used at that factory in the 18th century – this cornflower design was also used at the Duc d'Angoulême's Paris porcelain factory at the beginning of the 19th century. It has been copied by other European factories.

Willow Pattern

It is ironic that what is regarded as *the* blue and white pattern is a late 18th-century English pastiche. Usually attributed to Thomas Minton, the pattern was first made at the Caughley factory, but it has been extensively copied in Great Britain and China.

OTHER USEFUL TERMS

CELLULOID A thermoplastic material made from a mixture of cellulose nitrate and a plasticizer, usually camphor. It was popular for manufacturing handles for cutlery.

OVEN-TO-TABLE WARE Decorated casserole and serving dishes, in particular, that can withstand high temperatures, thus allowing the hostess to bake food in the dish and bring it straight from the oven to the table without being transferred into a serving dish.

STAINLESS STEEL A type of steel containing 12–15 percent chromium, making it resistant to corrosion. It has been the preferred metal for cutlery since the 1950s.

SERVING DISHES

The vegetable tureen (below), as well as the serving dish (opposite page) and the soup bowl, are all designed in a modernist shape typical of the period – the shape was directly inspired by American tablewares.

DINNER SERVICE

The table is set with Midwinter china in a pattern known as Nature Study, which was designed by Sir Terence Conran in 1954. The mixture of the matt black with the contrasting patterned white is an interpretation of the mix and match concept. The use of a transfer-print pattern, here depicting leaves, moths and butterflies, is a feature found on much china produced in 1950s Great Britain.

THE TABLE SETTING

The setting of this table is typical of one that would have been found in a middle-class house of the 1950s. The formal layout, despite its use of modern tablewares, reflects a rather traditional approach. It should not be forgotten, however, that oven-to-table ware was also popular, and people also tended to eat in a much more informal way with fewer courses, particularly if they were not serving guests.

THE POSTWAR ERA

As people and economies began to recover from the effects of War War II, including the huge cost, the move toward informality slowly re-emerged. In Great Britain the accession of a new queen to the throne in 1952 heralded what was described as a New Elizabethan Age. New discoveries were now being made in the scientific world, which led to developments in travel and communications. This interest in speed and science was reflected in the decoration of products made for the home, including tablewares, and ideas and trends that developed could quickly spread across the Atlantic in both directions.

Newly built housing differed from earlier homes: there was now a single reception room for sitting and eating instead of two separate rooms. Modern shapes have been appreciated during this era, but traditional patterns and forms continued to be made and to be popular as can be seen in A Focus on the Top 10 Patterns on pages 146–47.

CUTLERY
The cutlery was made by the British designer David Mellor. Arranged correctly on either side of the dinner plate, the setting is for soup, a first course and dessert. The second knife is for bread and butter.

THE PLACE SETTING
Included in this place setting is a dinner plate, with a soup bowl and its plate resting on it. Once the diner had enjoyed the soup, the soup bowl and plate would be removed, leaving the dinner plate ready to use. Sometimes, however, the dinner plate was used as a decorative service plate and would be removed, too – a custom that was established in restaurants. The side plate under the napkin is always placed on the left-hand side of the dinner plate.

FIFTIES PATTERNS

The United States emerged at the end of World War II as the dominant political and economic power. The story in Europe, where countries had to recover from the damage of war, was somewhat different.

In Great Britain the war still had to be paid for, and this led to many restrictions on the home market. For example, since 1941, the use of colours and patterns on china had been restricted on wares being sold in shops in the United Kingdom; however, to boost the economy, patterns were not restricted on wares that were made for exportation to other countries.

The British government lifted its restrictions in 1952 and there followed what can be described as a pattern boom. Emphasis on design had emerged in the mass market before the war: in the postwar era it bloomed. The Festival of Britain in 1951, with its focus on science and technology, led to the introduction of crystalline shapes and patterns on fabrics, furniture and tablewares.

Firms employed designers to produce a variety of patterns for them. The china manufacturer Midwinter employed the designers Terence Conran, Hugh Casson (who designed the Cannes and Riviera patterns) and Jessie Tait. Among the designers working for Foley China was Maureen Tanner, who was also a member of the Festival Pattern Group.

China manufacturers were not shy when it came to borrowing ideas from each other, and it was not uncommon to find similar patterns produced by different factories.

By the end of the decade, the Scandinavian idea of using texture as a pattern in both ceramics and metalwares had become established and was used by some of the British studio potters.

MIDWINTER PLATE, BOWL AND STAND

These pieces were made at the British Midwinter factory, which used many designers. Two designers are responsible for these pieces – one designed their shape, the other their pattern.

The plate is rimless and the bowl has a shaped wavy rim, both of which are in the shape designed by Roy Midwinter known as Fashion – which was based on the American Tomorrow's Classics range of wares designed by Eva Zeisel.

MIDWINTER STYLECRAFT CHINA

This set was manufactured by the Midwinter factory in their Stylecraft shape, which was designed in 1953. This shape was inspired by the organic ceramic shapes that were popular in the United States.

This 1955 pattern reflects the interest in molecular structures and science that had first been aroused by the 1951 Festival of Britain exhibition. The pattern is known as Festival and was designed by Jessie Tait, who worked for the factory and produced many abstract designs for them during this decade.

The name of the relevant designer is usually found on the bottom of a piece.

FOLEY CUP AND SAUCER

This bone china cup and saucer, made by Foley c.1956–57, is decorated with the London Pride pattern. It depicts a Lord Mayor and his swordbearer and coach outside the Guildhall. Two elegantly attired ladies look on. The pieces were designed by Maureen Tanner, and her name and that of the pattern are on the base of the pieces.

The tradition of using well-known designers and artists was established at the Foley firm in the 1930s when they commissioned people such as Graham Sutherland, Barbara Hepworth, Paul Nash and Milner Grey to create designs for them.

LORD NELSON WARE STACKING TEAPOT

The flowery decoration on this set is transfer-printed and is an example of a type of pattern known as chintz. It first appeared in the 1930s and remained popular for the following three decades. This example is in the Marina pattern and consists of a teapot, topped with a cup, and then a milk jug, on which the teapot lid sits.

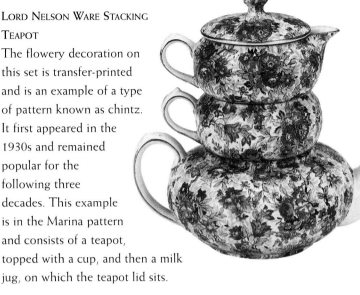

Although the cup and saucer are of conventional shape, the cup's handle reflects the interest in aerodynamic form at the time.

Polka dots had been used as a decorative motif in the 1930s and were popular again in the 1950s; they were also used on dress fabrics. This pattern is known as Red Domino and was designed by Jessie Tait in 1953. A Blue Domino version was also made.

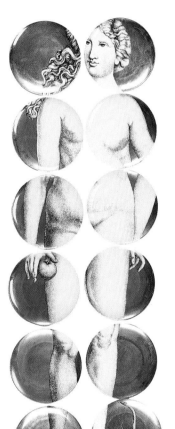

EVE, A SERIES OF 12 PLATES

These plates were designed by the Italian designer Piero Fornasetti in 1954 and, when placed together, they form a picture of Eve; there is a companion set of Adam. Fornasetti is well known for his surreal designs, which often borrow elements from antique engravings. He also designed the Themes and Variations set of dinner plates.

SIDE PLATE

The pattern on this side plate by Barker Brothers is typical of the wares made for the mass market. It is decorated with coffee pots, cutlery and other tablewares. Perhaps the best known of this type of decoration is the Ridgway firm's "Homemaker" pattern, designed by Enid Seeney, which depicts everyday furniture and household objects.

AERODYNAMIC SHAPES

I n the new atomic age that emerged during the postwar era in the 1950s, there was a preoccupation with science, as well as new developments in transportation. In the United States, these trends were incorporated into the designs of everyday household and commercial items, as can be seen in many of the electrical appliances from a typical American kitchen of the time and in the jukeboxes that were becoming increasingly popular in roadside diners – these items owe a debt to contemporary automobile designs.

The influence of speed that developed during the 1930s now grew into a much larger force. Advances in the design of planes and the breaking of the sound barrier heralded the jet age. In addition, science fiction grabbed the public imagination, and books and films with a proliferation of rockets and flying saucers became an intrinsic part of the 1950s. Indeed, by the end of the decade space travel had become a reality when the Russian man-made satellite Sputnik orbited the Earth for the first time.

All these events had an effect on contemporary design and influenced both the shapes and patterns of tableware. The new look proved to be a worthy rival to the organic and asymmetrical shapes that were also popular at the time.

Stainless steel was increasingly used for tableware such as cutlery. It was particularly suited to the elongated shapes that were being advocated as part of the decade's concentration on creating things new instead of imitating objects from the past.

OLD HALL STAINLESS STEEL PART TEA SET

These teawares are part of the Campden range, which was designed for Old Hall by Robert Welch and David Mellor, who designed the cutlery. The Campden range won the British 1958 Design Centre Award.

These pieces were made of stainless steel, an alloy that contains chromium and nickel, which makes it stain- and rust-proof. Stainless steel was first made in Britain in 1913. Initially, it was used for knife blades and then for cutlery and other tableware.

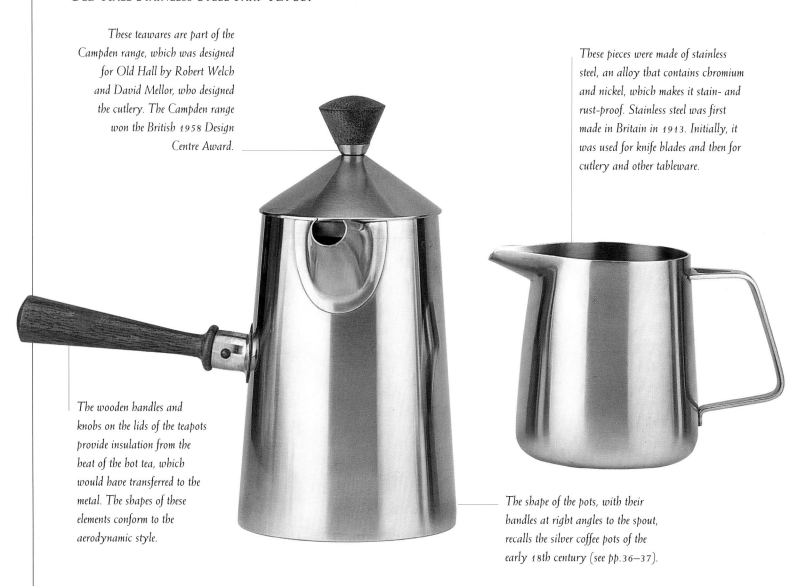

The wooden handles and knobs on the lids of the teapots provide insulation from the heat of the hot tea, which would have transferred to the metal. The shapes of these elements conform to the aerodynamic style.

The shape of the pots, with their handles at right angles to the spout, recalls the silver coffee pots of the early 18th century (see pp.36–37).

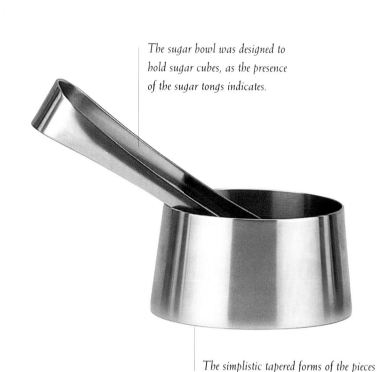

The sugar bowl was designed to hold sugar cubes, as the presence of the sugar tongs indicates.

The simplistic tapered forms of the pieces are typical of aerodynamic designs.

The shape of the spouts on the pots and the milk jug reflect the interest in the dawning of the jet age.

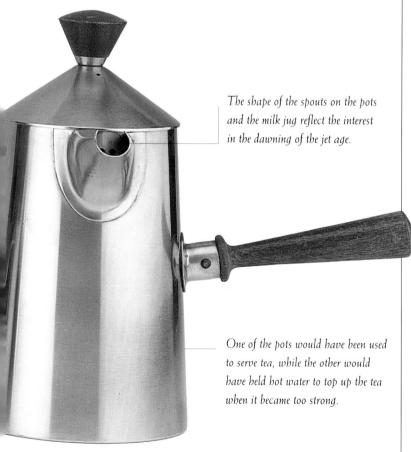

One of the pots would have been used to serve tea, while the other would have held hot water to top up the tea when it became too strong.

TEA SERVICE

These pieces come from a service manufactured in the 1950s – the design was created earlier by Eva Rottenberg for the Augarten factory in Vienna. The elegant flowing lines reflect the modern trends, and the elongated forms reflect the move to aerodynamic shapes. On the sugar bowl and teapot, the knops in the shape of a Chinaman's head add a whimsical touch.

VEGETABLE DISH AND COVER

A product of the British Burgess & Leigh factory, this circular dish was made for serving vegetables. At first glance, it may be thought to date from the 1930s, but its shape clearly reflects the interest in flying saucers. The firm made wares for both the domestic and export markets.

FLATWARE SERVICE

This set was designed by Arne Jacobsen and is made from stainless steel. The simplicity of the shape is highlighted by the long handles flowing into the "working" part of each item, such as the tines of the forks. They were made by the Danish Court jewellers A. Michelsen, indicating that stainless steel had arrived as a substitute for silver.

INFORMALITY

Although some informality in eating habits had become evident during the 1930s, it was the new social order that was ushered in after the war that brought huge changes. The era of the servant had finally passed: now the cooking and serving of a meal was done by the hostess, so meals and the items used to serve them became more simple.

At the same time, changes in domestic architecture saw the demise of separate sitting and dining rooms. Instead, the living room, where both functions could be fulfilled, became the norm for young homemakers. The idea of having a dining table in the kitchen also emerged, and guests soon became comfortable sitting and talking to their hostess while she prepared the food.

The new oven-to-table ware proved to be popular: as well as providing an aesthetically pleasing way of serving meals, it was also practical because there were fewer pans and dishes to wash afterward.

The idea of dropping in for coffee and a chat became a part of life, and the more formal cups and saucers were replaced by mugs, which like the china and other tablewares of the period, were often colourful or decorated with patterns. Practical commemorative mugs that could be used – instead of merely displayed in a cabinet – were made as mementos of places visited during a holiday or of special events.

Car ownership was becoming more widespread, especially in the United States. This led to more people going into the country, and so the picnic basket, fully equipped with plates, cups and cutlery, gained popularity. They had formerly been used by the more well-off, but were now produced in less expensive versions.

DENBY OVEN-TO-TABLE WARE

The Denby firm had first produced oven-to-table ware in the 1930s, but in 1956 they introduced the Greenwheat pattern. This was to be their most popular seller of the decade and remained in production until 1977.

The base bears the signature of the designer, Albert College. This was the first time Denby allowed a designer's name to appear on its wares. Because the wares stand on the kiln floor while they are being fired, the foot is not glazed.

These pieces were made from a type of stoneware that can withstand heat and were suitably decorated so they could go directly from the oven to the table.

The saucepan was made to go into the oven: stoneware should never be placed directly on a heat source such as a cooker ring.

DENBY MUGS

These three mugs are typical of those that became popular in the 1950s and 60s as a less formal container for tea or coffee. Made of stoneware, they were less likely to chip or break than china cups and saucers. The flower-patterned mug on the left probably dates from the late 1950s while the other two were made in the 1960s.

A range with a brownish tone rather than the green one seen here was made for the American market, where it was marketed under the name Harvest.

Each piece was hand-painted, therefore, small variations often appear in the design.

The pieces are (clockwise, from top right) a plate, gravy boat, lidded casserole, saucepan, meat plate and open casserole.

COFFEE JUG

This chrome vacuum jug – a relatively new entry into the market for coffee wares – was first manufactured by the American Thermos Bottle Co. in the late 1940s, and such jugs have been used ever since. The vacuum jug is popular when entertaining: because it will keep liquid at its original temperature, coffee can be made in advance and poured into the jug before the guests arrive.

PICNIC SET

Complete with metal vacuum flasks, this set contains all the typical items necessary for a picnic. Although this set dates from *c.*1930, it hints at the future popularity of picnic sets in the 1950s. With the exception of the flasks and cutlery, the items are made of plastic and are an example of Banda Lasta ware. The knife handles are made of celluloid.

WARES OF THE FUTURE

Tableware design has certainly changed in the last hundred years, and there are some almost timeless examples that will probably remain popular for their convenience or simple design. In a way, however, today's design ideas seem to be fairly static. Many of the post-modernist designers look back to the simple lines of the Bauhaus movement (see pp.132–33) and reproduce them, perhaps with subtle variations, but not really with a new concept.

Although the modern look is still in demand, there is a competing vogue for the old-fashioned, and many manufacturers have been producing china and silver that is often inspired by 18th- and 19th-century patterns. Even Gianni Versace's Medusa design for tablewares, which was first introduced in 1994, was inspired by the past — at least in their decoration, if not in their shape or colour.

The 1990s has seen a rise in the value and appreciation of the works of the studio potter and, perhaps, as with the Scandinavian designs of the 1950s, this is where new concepts for tableware will come from.

There is little doubt that among the new designers graduating from art schools there will be some with the potential to produce radically new designs, and others will have the vision to reinterpret earlier designs and forms in a new, exciting and vibrant way so that they, too, can become classics in the future.

LITTLE DRIPPER COFFEE POT

This coffee pot was designed by the architect Michael Graves for Swid Powell, an American ceramics company which specializes in producing post-modernist tableware in limited editions. Graves is also known for designing the bird-whistle tea kettle for the Italian firm Alessi.

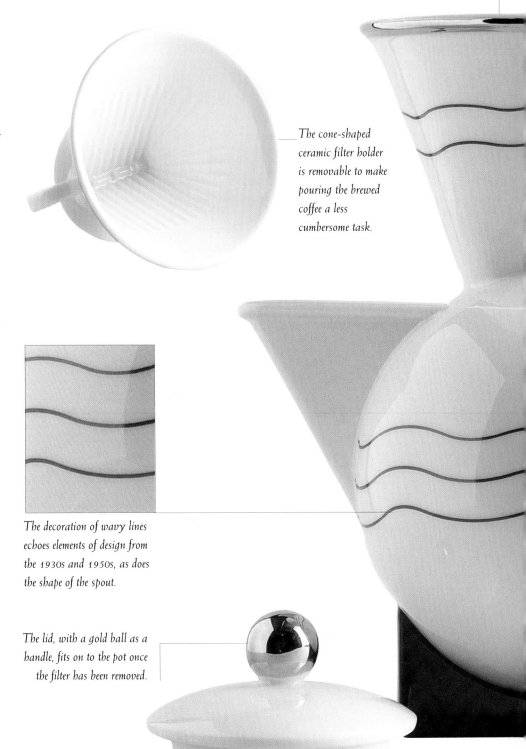

The cone-shaped ceramic filter holder is removable to make pouring the brewed coffee a less cumbersome task.

The decoration of wavy lines echoes elements of design from the 1930s and 1950s, as does the shape of the spout.

The lid, with a gold ball as a handle, fits on to the pot once the filter has been removed.

TEAPOT AND INFUSER

This teapot, which was made at the Rosenthal factory and is still in production, combines elegance and function with a minimum of decoration. It was designed by Walter Gropius, the leading figure in the Bauhaus movement, with Louis McMillen for Rosenthal's Studio Line in 1959.

DINNER SET

The spherical shape of this La Boule dinner service for four lends itself to a practical way of storing the pieces – the plates and bowls can be stacked into a ball to save space. Made from pottery, it was designed for Villeroy and Boch by Helen von Boch in 1971.

STUDIO TABLEWARE

One of the great studio potters of the 20th century, Dame Lucie Rie, made this group of glazed stoneware. The shapes are simple and elegant and have a sense of timelessness about them. Although these pieces are not decorated, some of Dame Lucie's wares have *sgraffito* decoration. Hans Coper, a notable potter, worked in Rie's London studio from 1946 until 1958; his work has a sculptural element.

The coffee pot was packaged with a set of instructions. If the original instructions have been retained with the coffee pot, the pot is considered more valuable.

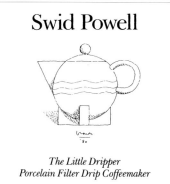

Swid Powell

The Little Dripper
Porcelain Filter Drip Coffeemaker

The coffee pot has been designed to be aesthetically pleasing with both the ceramic filter holder above the pot and with the lid in place (as can be seen on the instructions).

The round body of the coffee pot rests on an integral stand of four block feet.

INDEX

ACKNOWLEDGMENTS

t top, b bottom, c center, a above, bl below, l left, r right

4 Royal Pavilion, Brighton; 8 Rafael Vals Gallery, London/Bridgeman Art Library; 9 t Musée Conde, Chantilly/Lauros-Giraudon/Bridgeman Art Library, b Stapleton Collection/Bridgeman Art Library; 10 t Towneley Hall Art Gallery and Museum, Burnley, Bridgeman Art Library, b Private Collection/Bridgeman Art Library; 11 Forbes Magazine Collection, New York/Bridgeman Art Library; 22–5, 28–9 tr Christie's Images; 29 cr & br Jamestown Museum Collection, National Park Service, Colonial National Historical Park; 30–43, 46–53 c Christie's Images; 53 b Clive Corless/Marshall Editions; 54–9 t Christie's Images, 59 cl Christie's South Kensington, 59 cr Christie's Images, bl Peter Gaunt; 62–3 Christie's Images; 64–5 Goodwood House, by courtesy of the Trustees; 65 t–67, 72–3 Christie's Images, 73 t Christie's South Kensington, ca, cb & b Paul Atterbury; 74–5 Christie's Images; 75 t & b Paul Atterbury, c Christie's Images; 76–9, 82–3 Christie's Images; 84–5 Clive Corless/Marshall Editions, 85 t Christie's South Kensington, c & b Christie's Images; 86–7 Christie's Images; 90–1 Christie's South Kensington, 91 t Paul Atterbury; 92–97, 97 c & b Christie's Images, t Clive Corless/Marshall Editions; 98–9 Christie's Images, 99 t Christie's South Kensington, c & b Christie's Images; 102–3 Christie's Images, 103 t Christie's South Kensington, c Clive Corless/Marshall Editions, b Christie's Images; 104–5 Sotheby's Billingshurst; 105 t Christie's South Kensington, c & b J. Podlewski; 106–7 Christie's Images, 107 t & b Christie's Images, c Christie's South Kensington; 108–9 Christie's South Kensington, 109 tl, c & b Christie's South Kensington, tr Christie's images; 110–111 J Podlewski, 111 t & bl Christie's Images, c Peter Gaunt, br J. Podlewski; 112–3 Christie's South Kensington; 114–5 Christie's Images; 116–7 Richard Dennis; 120–1 Christie's South Kensington, 121 t Christie's Images, ca & cb Richard Dennis, b Clive Corless/Marshall Editions; 122–5 Christie's Images; 126–7 Christie's Images, 127 t Christie's South Kensington, c & b Christie's Images; 130–1 Christie's South Kensington; 132–3 Christie's Images, 133 t, c & b Sotheby's; 134–5 Sotheby's, 135 t Deco Inspired, c Katz Photolibrary, b Christie's South Kensington; 136–7, 140–1 Christie's Images; 141 t Christie's Images, c & b Christie's South Kensington; 142–3 twentieth century design; 143 t Deco Inspired, c RETRO home, b Betty Loving; 144–5 Christie's South Kensington; 145 t & c Sotheby's, b Christie's South Kensington; 146 t Christie's Images, cl Royal Doulton, cr Waterford Wedgwood, bl Christie's Images, br Royal Doulton; 147 t Spode, cl Zelli, cr & bl Christie's Images, br Paul Atterbury; 150–1 RETRO home; 150 Christie's South Kensington; 151 t & cr Christie's South Kensington, cl Tim Forrest, b Deco Inspired; 152–3 Christie's South Kensington, 153 t Christie's South Kensington, c RETRO home, b twentieth century design; 154–5 Betty Loving, 155 t Christina Donaldson, c Deco Inspired, b Henning Christoph/Katz Photolibrary; 156–7 twentieth century design, 157 t twentieth century design, c & b Christie's South Kensington.

If the publisher has unwittingly infringed copyright in any illustration reproduced, they would pay an appropriate fee on being satisfied as to the owner's title.

Chapter opener photography: Andrew Sydenham. Illustrations on pp. 26–7, 44–5, 60–1, 68–9, 80–1 and 100–1 by Kuo Kang Chen.

The publisher would like to thank the following for their help with the chapter openers: 28–9 Richard Young Antiques for wooden handled cutlery; 32–3 Burghly House; 48–9 Saltrum House; 70–1 and 88–9 Kate Dyson of The Dining Room Shop for ceramics and glass, Annie Boursot for silverware; 118–19 Abstract for glasses, Zeitgeist for wine coaster and sweetmeat stand; 138–9 Richard Dennis for ceramics, Georg Jensen for cutlery and glasses; 148–9 Richard Dennis for ceramics, David Mellor for cutlery.